HOW TO DRAW
MANGA

A STEP-BY-STEP GUIDE WITH OVER 750 ILLUSTRATIONS

HOW TO DRAW
MANGA

**EXPERT TECHNIQUES FOR CREATING YOUR OWN MANGA CHARACTERS
AND STORIES, WITH MORE THAN 50 EXERCISES AND PROJECTS**

TIM SEELIG AND YISHAN LI

southwater

This edition is published by Southwater,
an imprint of Anness Publishing Ltd,
Blaby Road, Wigston, Leicestershire LE18 4SE
info@anness.com
www.southwaterbooks.com
www.annesspublishing.com

If you like the images in this book and would like to investigate using them
for publishing, promotions or advertising, please visit our website
www.practicalpictures.com for more information.

Publisher: Joanna Lorenz
Editorial Director: Helen Sudell
Editor: Elizabeth Young
Cover Design: Oil Often
Production Controller: Christine Ni

Designed and produced for Anness Publishing Limited by Ivy Contract:
Project Editors: Hazel Songhurst, Sarah Doughty, Susie Behar
Designer: Glyn Bridgewater
Art Director: Lisa McCormick
Artists and Contributors: Yishan Studio, Rik Nicol, Wing Yun Man,
    Jacqueline Kwong and Tim Pilcher

ETHICAL TRADING POLICY
At Anness Publishing we believe that business should be conducted in an
ethical and ecologically sustainable way, with respect for the environment and
a proper regard to the replacement of the natural resources we employ.
    As a publisher, we use a lot of wood pulp in high-quality paper for printing,
and that wood commonly comes from spruce trees. We are therefore
currently growing more than 750,000 trees in three Scottish forest
plantations: Berrymoss (130 hectares/320 acres), West Touxhill (125
hectares/305 acres) and Deveron Forest (75 hectares/185 acres). The forests
we manage contain more than 3.5 times the number of trees employed each
year in making paper for the books we manufacture.
    Because of this ongoing ecological investment programme, you, as our
customer, can have the pleasure and reassurance of knowing that a tree is
being cultivated on your behalf to naturally replace the materials used to
make the book you are holding.
    Our forestry programme is run in accordance with the UK Woodland
Assurance Scheme (UKWAS) and will be certified by the internationally
recognized Forest Stewardship Council (FSC). The FSC is a non-government
organization dedicated to promoting responsible management of the world's
forests. Certification ensures forests are managed in an environmentally
sustainable and socially responsible way. For further information about
this scheme, go to www.annesspublishing.com/trees

PUBLISHER'S NOTE
Although the advice and information in this book are believed to be accurate
and true at the time of going to press, neither the authors nor the publisher
can accept any legal responsibility or liability for any errors or omissions that
may have been made nor for any inaccuracies nor for any loss, harm or injury
that comes about from following instructions or advice in this book.

The publisher would like to thank the following for kindly supplying photos for
this book: ALAMY: Japan Art Collection (JAC)/Alamy 6 (top), Paris Pierce/Alamy
6 (bottom), Interfoto Pressbildagentur/ Alamy: 7 (top), Jeremy Hoare/Alamy 10
(bottom left), Chris Willson/Alamy 11 (top), Digital Vision/Alamy 11 (bottom
right); BRIDGEMAN: 7 (bottom), CORBIS: John Van Hasselt/Corbis 10 (top),
Amet Jean Pierre/Corbis Sygma 9 (bottom left); Ferreol Murillo Fuentes 7 (right);
GETTY IMAGES: Getty Images/New Vision Technologies Inc. 11 (bottom left);
LAST GASP: Keiji Nakazawa 10 (middle); TOKYOPOP INC: 9 (bottom); VERTICLE
INC: 8 (both), 9 top.

Thanks to Pen to Paper, Lewes for providing the pen nibs and The Art Shop,
Wadhurst for supplying artist's materials for photography.

Previously published as part of a larger volume, *The Practical Encyclopedia
of Manga*

CONTENTS

The origins of manga

Whether you are a fan of manga or not, you will probably have read the headlines proclaiming its sweeping successes across the globe, noticed the titles creeping to the top of the bestseller charts, or seen teenagers on the bus reading the latest volume of *Naruto* or *Fruits Basket*. But what is manga, and what does 'manga' really mean? At its simplest level, it is the Japanese term for a comic book: the sequential fusion of illustrated panels and written dialogue. In practice, however, manga has come to represent a series of styles, subgenres and types of story that are recognized, and have been exported, all over the world. The popularity of manga is now at its peak, with bookshelves full of titles in every country in every conceivable genre, catering for every kind of reader, young and old. The greatest feature of manga is its universal accessibility: unlike Western comics, which have for several decades been perceived as the sole purview of young males reading about Spandex-clad superheroes, manga has been strongly embraced by girls and women. Manga as we know it may be a relatively new form of art, but its roots stretch back to the 17th century, birthed in a tradition of affordable, mass-produced prints that has been constantly evolving. Take the tour below to find out how it all began.

The birth of manga

The genesis of manga ties most closely with a form of mass-produced woodcut prints called *ukiyo-e*, or 'pictures of the floating world'. The 'floating world' refers to the blooming merchant class that gained a foothold in Japan from the 17th century onwards. Compared to traditional Japanese society, which was strongly governed by regulations and etiquette, the merchants were relatively unencumbered, and thus 'floating'. Ukiyo-e showed colourful scenes of urban life, from courtesans to sumo wrestlers; before long, it had expanded into rural landscapes, too. They were affordable, mass-produced and very popular. Ukiyo-e could also be found alongside text stories in picture books called 'ehon', another forerunner of modern manga.

One of the most famous and well-regarded artists of ukiyo-e, operating at the height of the Edo period (1603–1868), was a man named Hokusai. Born in 1760, Hokusai was painting by the age of six and published his first prints before 1780. He was among the first to use the term 'manga' in the title of one of his bound collections. His use of the word has been translated in dozens of ways: from 'whimsical pictures' to 'involuntary sketches', but it is clear that his concept was far from the one we know today.

◀ *Mishima Pass in Kai Province*, **by Hokusai**
Men surround the trunk of a tree in this example of Hokusai's work from 'Thirty-six Views of Mount Fuji', in which he travelled the Edo region c.1830 (modern-day Tokyo), illustrating the beloved volcanic mountain. The portfolio, created when he was in his seventies, was a popular and commercial success.

▲ *Coming from the Field*, **by unknown artist**
This ukiyo-e print demonstrates the shift from urban to rural concerns, as well as demonstrating the intricacy of line and vividness of colour for which the prints are famous. Note, too, the integration of descriptive text with the illustration – surely a precursor to caption boxes and word balloons.

From woodcut to cartoon

From Hokusai, it was not long before another significant development took place in the evolution of manga. Just as the woodcut method of ukiyo-e allowed great art to become available to those on moderate incomes, so the increasing prevalence of the industrial printing press and the daily newspaper – as well as Western influences in the Meiji era – took art and information to the masses. Newspapers opened the door for cartoonists and manga artists, first among them was Rakuten Kitazawa (1876–1955), revered as the founding father of modern manga. The first professional cartoonist in Japan, he did much to promote the art form by encouraging and promoting young manga-ka (artists) in the 1920s, and was instrumental to the success of the Sunday comic strip section *Jiji Manga*. Although Japanese comic strips could be found in newspapers and magazines from before the turn of the 20th century, it wasn't until the period after World War II that manga truly flourished.

The Great Wave off Kanagawa, by Hokusai ▲
This famous ukiyo-e print of a tidal wave dwarfing and reflecting the mountain beneath combines an intricate approach to wood-carved detail with a powerfully limited palette. Each colour would be applied to the print as a separate cut woodblock, with deeper shades needing several applications. Thus, while mass-produced, there was still a great deal of craft and time involved in every print.

◄ **Gestures of Daily Life, by Hokusai**
This colour woodblock print, from Hokusai's 'Manga' collection, tells a narrative of everyday urban life without the use of panel borders, in a manner that would be echoed by the forerunner of Western graphic novels, Will Eisner. Note how the composition of the figures guides the reader's eye down the page.

Caricature of Kitazawa ▶
This poster by the cartoonist Ferreol Murillo Fuentes (2005) was produced to mark the fiftieth anniversary of Kitazawa's death. Kitazawa's first cartooning jobs were for American publications: *Box of Curious* and *Puck*, both in the 1890s.

The rise of manga

Japan began its modernization at the beginning of the Meiji era in 1868, under the 45-year rule of the Emperor. During that time the country absorbed and perfected influences from the West. But it was in the years after World War II, when the country entered its most frenzied period of creativity and industrialization, that manga crystallized into the form we now recognize. A new generation of creators, who had grown up reading the comic strips of Kitazawa and his peers, embarked on their own manga careers. This time, their ambitions were greater: to use the medium to tell long-form stories, using all of the cinematic and artistic techniques at their disposal. The Japanese public fell in love with these new manga immediately, driving the weekly magazines in which they were contained to ever-greater heights of circulation success, and inspiring animated spin-offs, merchandise, de luxe collections – and imitators by the thousand. Magazines sprang up to cater for specific genders – shonen for boys, shojo for girls – and genre lines, too, were drawn.

Modern originator of manga

Dr Osamu Tezuka (1928–89), one of the young artists inspired in childhood by Kitazawa's work, fused his love of Japanese cartooning with the Western influences brought to Japan by the American occupying forces after the close of World War II. He took aspects of the cartoons of Walt Disney and fused them to a larger-than-life, cinematic storytelling, to create the dynamic, action-packed, 'big eyes, small mouth' style that has become synonymous with manga today. In his lifetime, he produced more than 150,000 pages of material – but his breakthrough hit, and most beloved character, was *Tetsuwan ATOM* (*Astro Boy*). Although much of his work has never been translated from the Japanese, Tezuka's influence on the development of manga cannot be underestimated. His work ranged from environmental fables (*W3/Wonder 3*), 'talking animal' stories (*Jungle Emperor/Jungle Taitei*), 'the mother of all shojo manga' (*Princess Knight/Ribon no Kishi*), sexually explicit historical epics (*Cleopatra: Queen of Sex/Kureopatora*), medical thrillers (*Black Jack*) and personal explorations of cosmic philosophy (*Phoenix*). Tezuka turned his pen to virtually everything. His last major manga epic (worked on between 1974 and 1984) was an eight-volume critically acclaimed retelling of the life of Buddha.

Tezuka's stylistic innovations which encompassed slow-motion progressions through panels, cinematic angles and plenty of rapid zooms from long to close-up shots – would go on to define much of boys', or shonen, manga over the next half century.

Effortless cool ▲
This panel from *Black Jack* showcases the medical anti-hero, just arrived by helicopter to perform another delicate operation.

◄ **The death of Buddha**
Buddha's mortal life and Osamu Tezuka's eight-volume epic come to an end in this touching crowd scene, as Buddha passes into nirvana surrounded by his friends, protégés and students. The end of the story represented 11 years of serialized work by Tezuka.

Birth of an epic ►
The cover for the first book in the English adaptation of the manga, designed by Chip Kidd, and split into eight translated volumes. The pages are presented in the 'flopped' format, where the original Japanese pages are mirrored so that the translation reads left to right.

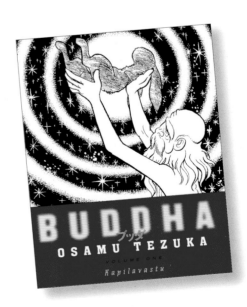

The evolution of shojo

Machiko Hasegawa (1920–92) was one of the first female manga artists to become a part of this new manga era, creating the massively influential strip *Sazae-san*, which began in 1946 and remains popular – as a weekly radio and animated television show – to this day. Her focus on the everyday life of women and girls crystallized into the broad tenets of shojo, or girls', manga. This revolution broadened the scope of manga yet again, and pointed the way towards the 'something for everyone' marketplace of today.

The year 1969 saw another sea-change, as the Year 24 Group (named for the year in which they were born: Showa 24, or 1949) of female manga-ka (a level of artistic expertise) made their shojo manga debut, shuffling perceived gender and genre restrictions and introducing many of the categories we see today, from romance to superheroines and shonen-ai (love stories between two boys, aimed at young girls) and shojo (including science fiction). The ascendance of the Year 24 Group also marked the first point at which the majority of manga for women and girls were being written and illustrated by their target demographic. They also pioneered the use of non-standard panel layouts, softening or removing panel borders, or changing them to suit the emotional tenor within, and altering the entire grammar of manga illustration as a result.

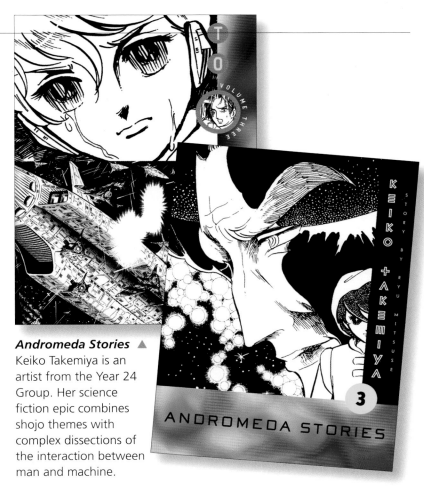

Andromeda Stories ▲
Keiko Takemiya is an artist from the Year 24 Group. Her science fiction epic combines shojo themes with complex dissections of the interaction between man and machine.

The manga format

Manga stories are usually serialized in 20-page chunks in bulky magazines. They are published weekly or monthly on low-quality paper to keep the cost down. The most popular series are subsequently collected in *tankubon*, which we would probably call graphic novels. The tight deadlines required by weekly or monthly publications producing tankubon mean that most manga-ka work in studios with a handful of (largely uncredited) assistants. These assistants aid in the drawing of backgrounds, and the shading and toning process. They also usually 'graduate' to manga-ka status, themselves within a few years.

Manga's massive appeal is often credited to the sheer breadth of its content. Modern manga tell stories of the fantastical, the futuristic, the romantic, and the humdrum. Whatever their age or interest, there will be a series out there for every reader.

Dragon Ball Z ▼
One of the most prolific shonen manga, the image below shows only a small selection from the series.

Fruits Basket ▲
The number one shojo manga in the English-speaking world, *Fruits Basket*'s enduring popularity rests on strong characters and a regular release schedule.

Manga worldwide

Manga is a multibillion dollar industry even within Japan, but its reach now extends around the world, whether literally, as in the swarms of reprints and original titles that can be found on English-language bookshelves, or metaphorically, as in the liberal borrowings of style made by entertainment industries in the West. Manga's greatest strength is in its flexibility: it is a format rather than a genre, a delivery mechanism rather than a prescription of content. Fans of giant robot action, high school romance, extreme cookery, basketball, monstrous dimensions, psychological horror, daring crime thrillers or illegal street racing can all find something that appeals to them on the bookshelves.

The manga invasion

One of the first manga to be translated and released in the West was Keiji Nakazawa's moving account of the Hiroshima bombing, *Barefoot Gen*. While other manga, such as *Lone Wolf and Cub*, were translated throughout the 1980s, it wasn't until the release of Masamune Shirow's *Appleseed* by Eclipse Comics and the recoloured edition of Katsuhiro Otomo's *Akira*, partially published by Marvel's EPIC imprint in 1988, that English-language demand for manga and anime began to grow, and the international market started to open up.

Throughout the 1980s and 1990s, series such as *Akira, Dragon Ball, Neon Genesis Evangelion, Pokémon, Oh! My Goddess, Ghost in the Shell, Battle Angel Alita, Love Hina, Ranama 1/2, Cowboy Bebop, Sailor Moon, Cardcaptor Sakura* and *Magic Knight Rayearth* saw increasing crossover success, bolstered by the twin assault of translated volumes and popular anime films and television shows.

Manga magazines ▼
Part of manga's attraction in Japan is its ubiquity: a wide selection of magazines covering all genres and tastes can be found in every bookshop, newsagent and train station kiosk.

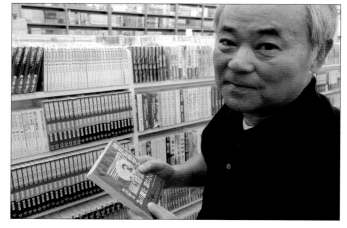

◄ **Keiji Nakazawa**
The author of *Barefoot Gen* browses his manga in a Hiroshima bookshop. Nakazawa began the semi-autobiographical, ten-volume series when his mother died of radiation poisoning, aged 60.

Post-nuclear holocaust ▲
Gen surveys the devastation in Hiroshima wraught by the atomic bomb dropped from the *Enola Gay*. *Barefoot Gen* deals with the harsh realities of life in the aftermath of an atomic explosion, from the initial devastation through to the more insidious effects of radioactive fallout. It ran in several mass-market magazines, from the early 1970s to the mid-1980s and has also been made into a television series and several animated films. *Barefoot Gen* was one of the first manga to be released in English from the mid-1970s.

Manga explosion

The period 1996–7 saw the founding of manga publisher TokyoPop by Mixx Entertainment with its headquarters based in California, USA. It was soon followed by a cadre of competitors, and the modern era of aggressively promoted tankubon collections began. Such companies often have thousands of volumes in print.

Although there are evergreen titles that retain their popularity indefinitely, there are always new young pretenders arriving to claim the most popular manga crown. In recent years, these have included the chilling supernatural procedural *Death Note*, the ninja-in-training epic *Naruto*, piracy quest *One Piece*, twentysomething drama *Nana*, martial arts expert *Ranma 1/2*, female cyborg Battle Angel Alita also known as *Gunnm*, the ghosthunting *Bleach*, gothic spectacular *Vampire Knight*, über-violent school satire *Battle Royale* and steampunk adventure *Full Metal Alchemist* but this is just dipping a toe in the pool.

Today, manga has truly conquered the world of comics, especially among younger readers, who have grown up fluent in its intricacies and culture-clash elements. Titles such as *Naruto* and *Fruits Basket* regularly displace all comers from the top of the *New York Times* bestseller list when a new volume is released.

Market leaders ▶
Manga today is made up of an array of newly translated titles and Original English Language (OEL) titles.

◀ **Manga merchandising**
As well as their enduring popularity as stories, the characters from many manga comics have become just as well known as pop culture icons, with *Astro Boy* (shown left) and *Hello Kitty* becoming phenomenal international sales successes in clothing, toys, bags and more.

Using this book

This book aims to make you a master of manga, able to turn your hand, pen or digital stylus to any one of the numerous manga genres, confident in your storytelling and draftsmanship abilities. The chapters to come will give you the opportunity to sample every style of manga, from contemporary shojo to futuristic shonen and all points in between. As you work your way through the book, or simply dip in and out, you'll find an array of helpful hints, tips and short cuts, in-depth walkthroughs of techniques, explanations of terms, materials and approaches. There are unique projects to test your understanding and ability, while giving you the opportunity to show off all that you've learned, all clearly illustrated by colourful examples from a professional manga-ka. Whether you're a manga novice or an experienced illustrator and writer, you'll find something new here to challenge and inspire.

◀ **Skateboader**
Manga thrives on energetic protagonists, blistering action and colourful settings: so maximize your potential over the next few chapters.

Cyborgs and androids ▲
Manga is an opportunity to let your imagination run wild: follow the guides and you'll soon have dozens of fully populated worlds to choose from.

Styles of manga

There are many styles of manga around today, although some of the lesser-known genres don't make it over to Europe or the USA. Unlike comics in the West, manga in Japan is a national form of entertainment, and much like novels and films, covers just about every aspect of life. Some manga is purely fantastical and escapist, while other genres are centred around more realistic or educational themes. The genres listed here don't encompass the entirety of the manga scene – the more extreme forms are not covered – but this overview will provide you with a good idea of what's possible in your own work by showing you what is currently practised and popular in the world of manga.

Core genres

Like other art forms, manga is grouped into genres according to common attributes. Stories which share similar elements and characters are usefully defined in this way. There are four core genres, as defined by the gender and age of their target readership. These include manga for children, for young people (divided into stories for both girls and boys) and mangas for adults in all sorts of possibilities and varieties. The core mangas are:

Kodomo ▶

This genre is aimed at the very young (*kodomo* means 'child') and based on humour. Sometimes the stories have no dialogue, so children who can't read get everything they need from the visuals.

Kodomo has its own traits that distinguish it from other genres:
1. Child protagonists who usually have cute, intelligent pets.
2. Humorous storylines.
3. Simple narratives with easy themes that can be understood by as wide an audience as possible.

Shonen ▲

This is the most popular type of manga worldwide, largely because it is these stories that get translated and exported. Shonen is aimed at boys aged between 12 and 18 (*shonen* means 'boy') and thrives on constant, over-the-top action, adolescent male heroes seeking to be the best they can be, and quest-based narratives, structured almost like video games, with frequent 'boss battles' and 'levelling up'.

◀ **Shojo**

Meaning 'young girl', between 7 and 18 years old, *shojo* concentrates on emotion and feelings. Originally drawn by men, an explosion of female artists in the 1970s brought a sea-change in subject matter. Shojo stories share young female leads, themes of romance and friendship, and thought-provoking, not punchy, dialogue.

◀ **Seinen and josei**

Aimed at adults, seinen was first developed in the 1960s for men aged between 18 and 25, but its readership has expanded to men in their forties and beyond. Josei is targeted at women aged over 20.

Most seinen and josei stories share the following traits:
1. Protagonists in positions of authority: heads of companies, the armed forces, and so on.
2. More realistic, less exaggerated characters.
3. 'Cinematic' dialogue, lending the stories a filmic quality.
4. Sporadic use of comedy.
5. Adult themes, including realistic violence and erotica.

Manga subgenres

Within the four main genres, there are various subgenres aimed at specific audiences within each defined age and gender group.

Gakuen ▲
This means 'high school': appropriately, all of the stories take place within the confines of a school and are part of the shojo genre.

Ronin ▲
This is a seinen manga featuring a rogue, 'masterless', samurai warrior. The warrior wanders ancient Japan, working only for those who meet his price, or defending the innocent. His reputation instils fear, loyalty and awe.

Mahokka ▲
This means 'magical girls', and is a shojo comic featuring girls endowed with magical powers who fight evil. Stories start in high school, but often leave for more fantastic locations.

Lady comic ▶
A subgenre for women, part of josei. Target readers of lady comics are women in their twenties, especially home or office workers. Stories reflect the lives of their readers, spiced up with romantic meetings and secret dates between aspiring lovers. It is the 'daytime soap' of manga.

Jidaimono ▲
Part of shonen or seinen. The protagonists of jidaimono are ninja or samurai-style characters. Stories are typically epic and set in historical Japan. They may be based on actual events.

Sentai ▲
Stories based on shonen or seinen genre. They are similar to jidaimono, but usually have a mythical edge, utilizing the full breadth of Japanese folklore, from demons to ancestral gods. The protagonists often have special, even magical abilities.

Cyberpunk and mecha ▲
Both are science fiction settings. Cyberpunk showcases futuristic (even fetishistic) technology, often with cyborg (cybernetic organism) protagonists. Cyberpunk is a subgenre of seinen while mecha is closer to shonen. Mecha characters are usually pilots of enormous, man-shaped robots, defending the planet against a similarly giant alien threat. Common threads in both genres are the blurring of the boundaries between man and machine, and the difficulty of halting technological advancement, should it fall into the wrong hands.

Spokon ▲
This means 'sporty spirit' and is a subgenre of shonen or shojo. The shojo heroine has to make an arduous and demanding journey, as she strives to become the best at her chosen sport.

Tools of
the trade

It is relatively straightforward to achieve professional manga results with the aid of a few basic tools. Here is a chance to familiarize yourself with the array of pencils, pens, tones and colours available, plus some examples of their associated techniques.

Pencils

What we draw with is as important as what we draw on. By experimenting with as many different tools as possible, you will discover what best suits your way of working. The pencils shown below are all suitable for drawing manga, but your choice needn't be confined to these.

The majority of manga are illustrated in black and white, so your everyday toolkit should consist of standard pencils, perhaps divided into 'line-making' and 'tone-making' types. If you are planning to ink your pencil lines for later

reproduction or colour, for instance, you may find that using an HB pencil or mechanical pencil to lay down your lines may be all you need, with line weight provided later by brush or dip pen, and tone or colour added digitally. Water-soluble pencils and charcoal sticks are best confined solely to the colour and shading portions of your work. Alternatively, you may wish to ink your pencil lines, erase all of your initial 'construction marks', and add shading with softer-leaded pencils to retain a more organic, traditional-media feel.

Types of pencil

HB pencil

2B pencil

4B pencil

0.7mm mechanical pencil

2mm mechanical pencil

Blue pencil

The pencil is an artist's most versatile tool, with an extensive choice available from hard and grey to soft and black. 'H' refers to hardness and 'B' to blackness. B to 9B are the soft, black choices. HB falls right in the middle and is the best general-purpose pencil. 2H to 9H are the hard pencils in the spectrum, with 9H the hardest. Their more permanent marks score the paper, making them more difficult to erase.

You may wish to invest in three levels of blackness: for example an HB, a 4B (very soft, very black), and perhaps a 2B (soft and dark grey). Pencil thicknesses also vary and your choice will depend on whether you want loose or precise lines. A selection of pencils to fit a standard pencil-sharpener are probably the most useful.

The tip of a mechanical pencil retains a consistent thickness: it blunts equally and never requires sharpening. A lead size of 0.5mm will produce fine lines, but snaps easily. A 2mm lead is resilient, but your lines will be less precise. A 0.7mm lead is perfect for both fine detail work and constant pressure. Mechanical pencils are excellent for manga creators who ink their pencil lines, as they allow for quick rendering without sharpening breaks. They are less useful for shading, as it's impossible to shade large areas with the side of a mechanical lead, or vary the line weight through pressure and alteration of angle.

Many artists use a blue pencil to sketch out ideas or block in proportions because blue doesn't show up when scanning line work in black and white or greyscale. An artist creates initial layouts in blue, then uses an ordinary pencil to go over the marks they want to keep. It is important not to press too hard when using a blue pencil to avoid marking the paper.

Blue pencils ▶
The basic proportions and details of a figure are laid down in blue pencil first, roughing in the position of the character on the page. Standard pencils are drawn over the top, cutting down on the usual amount of erasing and reworking.

Erasers

A good eraser is essential, as you're bound to make errors or change your mind as you draw. You can also use an eraser to add highlights, rubbing out areas of shading to let the white of the paper show through. Most erasers are rubber, which can leave residue on the page or tear the paper. An alternative is a malleable putty rubber, which leaves no residue, and also erases softer pencil lines. Don't use a putty rubber to erase large areas of drawing, as they quickly become warm, which leads to smearing of marks.

Eraser   Putty rubber

Mark-making

The term mark-making describes putting your pencil to paper and observing and controlling how the pencil reacts. Try your mark-making with a variety of pencils. Create as many types of lines as you can – straight or spiral lines, shading, shapes etc – and think about how these could be applied to your drawing. Create a library of the marks that are most appealing to you.

Manga illustration is all about the use of thin, open and precise line work – 'cartoony' areas left open for tone or colour. With that in mind, the most common mark you make will be a simple line: curved, straight or a mixture of the two. Finding a pencil that sits comfortably in your hand, and a lead that doesn't blunt or snap too quickly is half the battle.

Shading is where mark-making comes into its own, as shown by the examples below. Simple ways to vary your shading include pressing harder with the tip of the pencil to produce lines of increasing thickness as the pencil tip blunts (too much pressure will break the lead). Using the side of the pencil produces a thick line immediately, which also increases with pressure.

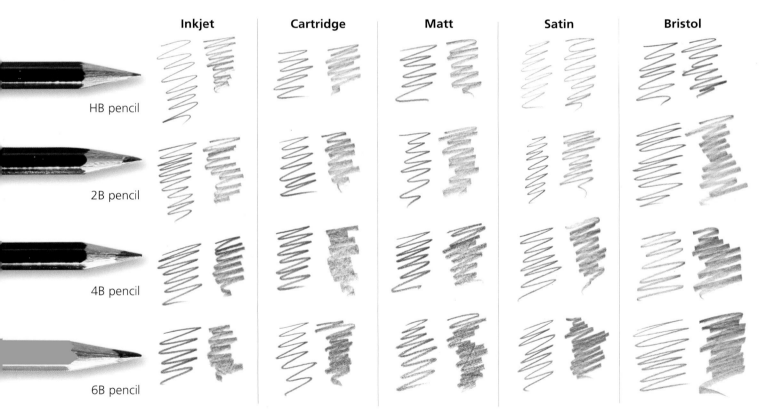

| | Inkjet | Cartridge | Matt | Satin | Bristol |

HB pencil
2B pencil
4B pencil
6B pencil

Water-soluble pencils ▶
While not useful for everyday pencilling, water-soluble pencils literally blur the line between pencils and paints, creating impressionistic tone and colour effects.

Pencil-on-paper effects ▲
These marks show how the choice of paper and pencil affect your drawing line. You'll see how different marks suggest themselves for different purposes – from easy-to-erase pencils ready for inking to softer shades perfect for the line work on a watercolour cover.

Pens and inking

Inking is what is meant by putting the final lines on the page. This is what you do once you have laid down your pencil lines and are ready to commit to the art you have created. Inking over your pencil marks will make them bold and clean; suitable for scanning, reproduction and print.

If you are inking by pen, you can begin with something as humble as an everyday rollerball. The professional choice is either a dip (nib) pen or a technical pen (a Rotring or equivalent). Dip pens suggest greater depth than technical pens, as you can vary the line widths by applying pressure to the nib. The lighter you press your nib on the page, the thinner the line; the harder you press the nib, the wider you'll force its prongs, creating a thicker line. Technical or fineliner pens, on the the other hand, produce consistent results and are easier to use. You don't need to replenish their ink supply every few marks, and can worry less about blotting. If you rest a dip pen in one place you will soon have a blob of ink on the page, but technical pens are not nearly as free-flowing.

Types of pen and nib

Dip pens ▼
Look closely at an example of published manga and you will notice a variety of depth in the finished lines. Lines will often start thick and end much thinner, which is achieved by changing the pressure exerted on the pen. Dip pens require dipping ink and the ink has to be replaced after every few strokes. However, the ink is considerably more resilient to light and the erasing process than that in a technical or fineliner pen. Don't try using a fountain pen as the ink that comes in standard cartridges is not of sufficient quality.

Technical pens ▼
Many operate using ink refill cartridges, giving long-lasting consistency of line in a wide variety of thicknesses, though you cannot alter the thickness of the line while drawing. Be aware that the ink in some pens may be picked up or 'greyed' when erasing, giving spotty results when scanned.

Rollerballs and fineliners ▼
Traditionally handwriting pens, these disposables can provide a clean technical line in an instant, and are often useful for touching up areas of black after erasing pencil lines and finding you've missed a spot. They have relatively slow drying times, however, which can lead to smearing.

Technical pen

Technical pen

Rollerball pen

Fineliner pen

Nibs ▼
Pen nibs come in a wide variety of shapes and sizes, and finding the most effective ones for your work is largely a process of trial and error.

Round nib ▲
Suited to all types of line work, a round nib is the most versatile. The width of the lines produced will vary depending on the pressure that is applied.

Turnip nib ▲
Easy to use and can achieve lines of various thicknesses. However, it lacks the flexibility to adjust with pressure and is often used for making even lines.

G nib ▲
This type of nib also lacks flexibility, and is used to produce steady thick lines. It holds more ink than a turnip nib, so can be useful for ruling in panel borders.

Inking

Drawing with a dip pen is a knack that requires practice. Once you get used to handling the pen, however, the results are easy to appreciate.

How you hold your pen is important. Grasp it close to the nib to increase stability. The farther up the shaft you hold the pen, the more your lines will wobble, and the less control you will be able to exert. The angle at which you hold your pen is also important: ink is drawn on to the page through surface tension, so there's no need to hold your pen perfectly upright. Treat it almost as you would a pencil, but remember that the shape of the nib and its prongs make it easier to draw a stroke from the top down to the right (rather than to the left) or from the bottom up to the top. Rotate your paper, or alter your technique, to prevent nib-skipping and ink spatter.

Dipping the pen

The golden rule is to keep the pen as free from excess ink as possible. If your pen comes out dripping, you've got too much. You will get beading, or strokes that are too thick at the beginning of a line. It's important to keep your ink flow even and predictable.

One way to do this is to decant ink into a separate inkwell, up to a level where you can almost touch the bottom without submerging the pen beyond the nib. This ensures you draw an equal amount of ink each time you dip. Preventing ink from reaching the pen's shaft also stops stray droplets from falling on to the nib.

Alternatively, keep a scrap of paper or card (preferably the same kind as you are working on) to test ink consistency by drawing a line every time you dip your pen. You can shake excess ink on to the scrap as well.

Tip: Don't become too fixed or rigid in your adoption of one form of pen over another. Many artists use a combination of both dip and technical pens – dip pens for organic, natural elements and technical or fineliner pens for backgrounds and inanimate objects.

Pens in practice ▼
These two drawings show the same character illustration made with different pens. The left used a dip pen, the right used a fineliner pen.

Dip pen

Fineliner pen

Brushes and paper

You can also use brushes to ink your work. It's not as fast a process as using a pen, but it produces a smoother result, particularly when it comes to curves. A brush can also hold more ink than a dip pen, which makes for longer lines without returning to the inkwell. In short, the brush is a far more flexible inking tool, but it takes more practice to master. A brush also needs more care and attention than a pen. A dip pen has only one nib, whereas a brush has innumerable, far more flexible and delicate components. The head of the brush, or 'tuft' as it's otherwise known, is made from animal hairs or synthetic fibres, and needs to be kept in good condition. Don't move your brush abrasively against the paper, or you will disrupt the hairs, which will detract from your ability to keep lines clean and even. More importantly, clean the brush thoroughly after every use, reshape the tuft while wet, and store your brushes tuft-up when not in use.

Tufts

A brushhead or tuft comes in various shapes and sizes and is held in place by a metal clamp or ferrule. In the same way that you select a nib, your choice of tuft will depend on the effect you want. For manga inking, you'll need a relatively thin, round tuft, or a small selection thereof. Below are the most common tuft types.

Brushstrokes ▶
This composite image shows only a small sample of the type of marks possible with a single brush – from wash effects to fine strokes. Note how just one tuft can create a wide variety of strokes depending on the pressure applied, the angle of attack and the amount of ink on the brush.

Rounds ▼
This tuft is a cylinder of hair that stretches down to a point. Like the round nib, it is the most generally applicable of all the tufts as it can be used to apply ink in both thin and broad strokes. Challenge yourself to ink an entire page using just one thickness.

Flats ▼
This tuft is square with a flat end. It is useful for filling in large areas of colour and for making wash effects. If used on end, held at a right angle to the page, it can also produce steady thin lines with the tuft held at the correct angle.

Filbert ▼
This triangular-shaped tuft is halfway between a flat and a round. It starts off flat but tapers to a point, meaning that by varying pressure you can create lines that taper from thin to thick, vice versa, or any point in between. It works best at larger sizes.

Fan ▼
A fan brush has a thin layer of bristles spread out by the ferrule. It is used to lay down parallel lines of ink by holding the brush end-on, at right angles to the page, often with a nearly dry tuft. It is useful for applying certain hatching and shading effects.

Brush sizes

Brushes come in varying sizes, each with a given number. You only need a small selection: some small rounds for detail work; a larger brush for filling areas. The number corresponds to the circumference of the ferrule. There is no international numbering system or standard measurement the industry must follow, and size varies between manufacturers. You should be able to find equivalents to your favoured brush sizes anywhere in the world.

Brush selection ▶
An assortment of brush sizes like this will in all likelihood be quite sufficient for your manga career. Art shops will often sell combination packs of brushes, or you can assemble your own selection based on personal preference. The variety is extensive and can include natural and synthetic bristles.

The correct ink

Whether you ink with a dip pen or a brush, or more likely a mixture of the two, the only ink you should use is Indian ink, the lifeblood of comics illustration. Unlike other types of ink, Indian ink contains shellac, so it is resistant to wear and tear (particularly the kind caused by rubbing out pencil marks) and it dries very quickly.

This fast-drying ability is precisely why it can't be used in fountain pens, because it would soon cause a blockage. This is why it's important to thoroughly clean tools after you finish working – so rinse your brushes and pens under water. Washing-up liquid can help keep pen nibs and brushes clean, but be sure you rinse it all off before drawing again.

Tip: Blotting paper can be handy to clean up small spills, and a small container of water will keep tools clean while you work. A piece of scrap paper of the same specification you are drawing on will allow you to experiment with the way your brushes and pens will react before you attempt your final piece.

Different types of paper

Nib

Brush

The five papers described here can all be used for manga. There are many other papers, but as manga is usually laid down in pencil and ink on to white surfaces, these are the most suitable.

Inkjet paper
This paper is thin, and when saturated with ink can begin to 'cockle' (crease). It's also easy to inflict damage with your eraser. Inkjet is cheap, and can withstand pencils and inks making it ideal for practice and sketching.

Cartridge paper
A thick, heavy paper, preferred by many artists and illustrators, originally used for making cartridges in weaponry.

Matt finish paper
Smooth finish is great for brushwork. Ink dries quickly, but you'll need a lot of white gouache to cover errors.

Satin finish paper
Use a rollerball rather than a dip pen. A good choice if you are inking by brush, although large areas of black brushmarks may appear inconsistent. Satin finish paper takes longer to dry than matt.

Bristol board
This paper is thick, with a smooth finish suitable for inking, making it the industry standard for comic illustrators. Holds ink well and allows for easy erasing: it's tough enough to be sent worldwide without too much in-transit creasing.

Tone

Adding tone is about adding weight to your drawing. You are essentially adding marks in different ways, whether that means adjusting the width of the lines, the length, or how light or dark they are. Tone adds dimension, mood, shade, atmosphere and texture to a drawing. You can practise its application by making sketches of your work on sheets of tracing paper. Once you've created a few examples, you can pencil different versions of tone and overlay them on your final piece. When you come to the final inking stage, pick the example that strikes you as the most effective.

There are various methods of applying tone. One classic example is cross-hatching – parallel shading lines that cross over one another. Another example of tone is washing, or using diluted black ink to apply grey shades. Washing is more subtle than hatching, and will soften the look of the final piece, diminishing the hardness of the main inks. Ultimately, the toning you choose will depend on the mood or genre of your story. If your story is light-hearted, for example, you are likely to confuse the reader by including large areas of shadow and may wish to avoid significant toning altogether.

Examples of tone

The following examples demonstrate how lines drawn in various ways create varying tones. Some styles have been used more than once, but in different combinations. All of the toning methods here are based on layering lines over one another – with the denser regions being the darkest, and areas of light being shown by an absence of tone. In any given image, you may find yourself using a variety of these tones to provide different textures to the hugely various human, animal, vegetable and mineral inhabitants of your manga artworks.

> **Tip:** Match tones with objects: scribbled, organic lines for people or clothes; rigid hatches or shiny stipples for technology.

Short lines ▲
Shading is built up by overlapping short lines drawn in the same direction.

Dots ▲
Fairly evenly spaced dots suggest light and shade through their relative density.

Cross-hatching ▲
Straight lines cross over one another to create mesh-like patterns. The denser the lines, the darker the area.

Spray stippling ▲
A scattergun approach creates rough areas of light and shade, again dependent on the density of marks.

Short lines ▲
Shadowed areas are tightly packed with lines, almost overdrawn.

Dots graduated ▲
Dots can be drawn closer together or made larger to suggest greater darkness.

Cross-hatching ▲
Hatches can be overdrawn to create darker areas, or the meshes further contracted.

Spray stippling ▲
A spray approach to shading is excellent for replicating stone and brickwork.

Short lines ▲
Shadows are built up in layers, working from the outer rim towards the highlight.

Dots graduated ▲
Dots become larger and more tightly packed the farther they are from the impact of light.

Cross-hatching ▲
Again, overdrawing suggests dimensionality. You may want to use an eraser to create white highlights.

Spray stippling ▲
Shadows are stippled on in increasingly stronger layers to provide a contrast between areas of light and shade.

Using tone

Adding tone appropriately will increase the effectiveness of your drawing and your story. But it is important to understand what you are trying to achieve beforehand, particularly since there are so many possibilities at your disposal. The example shown here illustrates how different shading techniques can be created using lines and areas of solid black, and how different tones can be integrated into the same image.

Tones in practice ▶

Dramatic results can be achieved with your line work by combining a number of different toning effects. Approach each of your tones as a texture in your artistic arsenal. Here, cross-hatching and dots capture two different fabrics, some spray stippling brings the hair to life, and an array of short lines behind the character create a hazy night scene or a paparazzi-stalked premiere.

Though all of one tonal strength (save the highlights), the texture adds interest to the hair without distracting from the line work.

The short lines and large highlight areas suggest both a background and an emotional state, while still throwing the focus forward on to the woman.

Ink-washing

If you are still experimenting with ink-washing, you may wish to work from a photocopy of your finished inks, as it is difficult to make corrections to your shading once you begin.

The principle behind ink-washing is simple: by mixing your Indian ink with varying percentages of water, you can apply (with a brush) consistent, strong and long-lasting greytones. You'll need to experiment with the mixtures of course (start with one part ink to one part water as a mid-tone, and add or subtract water and ink from there), and decant your ink into a suitable palette or container, but the actual act of washing is the same as painting, only in greyscale. You'll find that layers of shading can be built up by overwashing a light grey section a second, third or fourth time.

Washes in practice ▶

Ink washes add a more naturalistic, painterly effect to your finished lines, adding in a human touch that pre-cut or computer tones can sometimes lack.

Darker areas are built up in layers. The inexact mixtures of tones create a dreamier, fogbound quality.

Darker areas are painted over a mid-tone in successive washes. Highlights are left as white paper.

Colour

Despite advances in printing technology, and the increasing availability of high-level digital colouring packages, the vast majority of manga are still printed in black and white for reasons of cost and time effectiveness. Thousands upon thousands of books and weekly magazines are printed every month, usually on cheap paper. The absence of colour also gives many anime adaptations an extra edge, as fans of a manga book series finally get the opportunity to see their favourite characters in full-colour action. That does not mean there aren't any opportunities for colouring your work, or even that you should not pursue a full-colour manga story. Promotional purposes and cover art for your manga will be the most obvious venues, so it's worth knowing the colouring basics, as you'll never know when an opportunity might arise. Given the increasing popularity of comics on the Internet, you may find that the only way to grab attention for your creation is to release it in full, anime-challenging colour. The majority of comics today are coloured digitally, using packages like Adobe Photoshop, but the principles of colour are the same, whether using traditional or digital media.

Paints, inks and dyes

Walking into any art store will provide you with a thrilling and bewildering array of colouring choices. Paints such as these offer a range of bold ways to tint your manga illustrations.

Watercolour paint ▶
Available in two forms: pans, which are compressed blocks of colour that need to be brushed with water in order to release the colour, and tubes of moist paint. Watercolours seldom have a natural white; white is created by leaving areas of the paper unmarked, and lighter shades created by thinning the paint with water.

Gouache paint ▶
Soluble in water, allowing you to make alterations, gouache may crack when dried. The natural white can be used as a corrective.

Acrylic paint ▶
A brighter finish than gouache, acrylics have a stronger sense of colour. Soluble in water, so just as versatile as gouache, they can also be mixed with gouache for a watercolour finish.

Watercolour dyes ▶
Similar to watercolour paints, dyes give even brighter results. They are used for more 'in your face' productions, as dyes are very intense – perfect for manga with high energy and bright colours. Dyes also have a high tolerance to exposure from direct sunlight.

Watercolour paint in tubes   Watercolour paint in pans

Gouache paint   Acrylic paint

Watercolour dyes

Pencils and markers

Colouring pencils ▼
Available in soluble and non-soluble varieties. Blend colours with cross-hatching or a subtle fade from one complementary tone to another. An affordable alternative to paints or inks, they tend to suffer when digitally reproduced.

Markers ▶
Coloured markers are the staple of traditional-media manga colouring. The technical ability of the artist very much controls the success of the outcome. In good hands they reproduce well, remain bright, don't bleed on the page or combine unfavourably with Indian ink. They come in a wide range of shades. You can combine two or even three nibs into a single pen, and they can be overlaid to produce darker shades of the same colour, or can be easily blended with other hues.

Using colour

Adding colour is an excellent way to add a new dimension to your creations, whether on the cover of your manga or on a pin-up. A single colour image of your cast can 'resonate' through your entire story, even if the rest of the pages are in black and white. Give your central character bright green hair on a cover and that character's hair will 'read' as green throughout the rest of the story.

The colour wheel ▶
Every colour has a complementary opposite. Combine complementaries for more pleasing compositions.

The colour wheel shows the gradients of each tone, from light to dark, in each hue.

Some colours 'jar' in interesting ways when placed next to one another: purple and orange, red and blue, for example. Try out these if you want an unsettling or eye-burning effect on your manga page.

Colours directly opposite are complementary: red and green, blue and orange, purple and yellow etc.

Try creating your own colour wheel with your chosen medium, and practise blending and mixing colours to achieve the required variances in tone.

Colour in practice

Each traditional media has different techniques to master, and only by experimenting will you be able to find a colouring style that suits you. The basics, however, are shared by all. Pencils, markers and paints should all be laid down lightly on the first 'pass', leaving highlighted areas empty so that the white of the paper shows through. After demarcating highlights, add a mid-tone of your chosen colour, and add areas of shadow by going over this tone with the same pencil or marker a second or third time.

Complementary colours ▶
The deep green of the hair draws our attention to the central characters, while the fiery orange-red borders the image and maintains that sharp focus.

Uses a limited colour palette. Notice how the background and hair are reflected in the skin tones and dress detailing.

The white of the paper is left to shine through as an extreme highlight.

The deep green of the hair is in complementary opposition to the dark red.

How to draw a manga character

The manner in which characters are drawn is the main feature of how manga, or any type of comic strip, works. A reader has to identify each character in a story on every panel – after all, it's the characters that are going to carry the majority of the narrative from page to page.

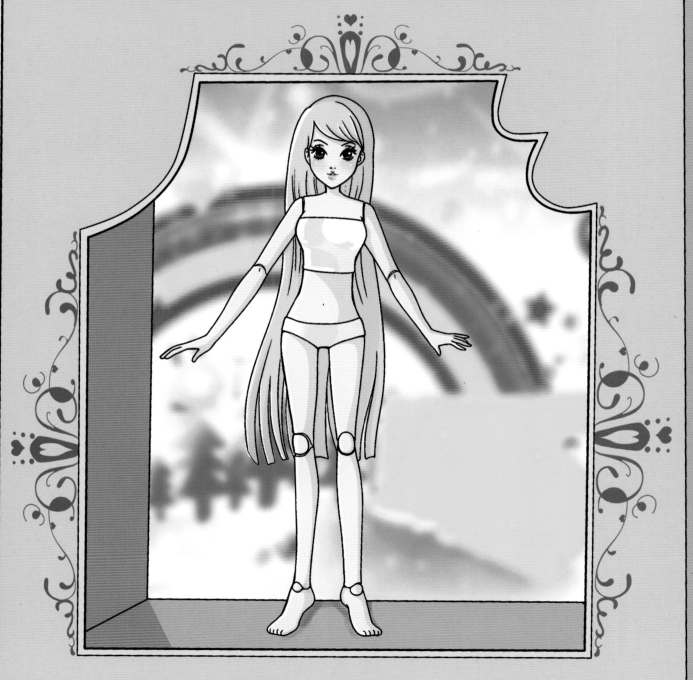

Heads and faces

There are set rules to designing manga characters, which include specific guidelines on the drawing of heads, faces and specific features, such as eyes, noses and mouths. The rules vary according to a character's gender, age, and moral alignment (good or evil). The way you draw a female villain's eyes, for instance, will be different from the way you design the eyes of an heroic male figure. In both of these cases, your design will be based on the application of some simple rules.

Within this framework, an experienced manga artist will show their own style and characteristic techniques. In time, you will also develop a unique way of interpreting these rules. It makes sense to start with the basics of head and face drawing. The practice exercises in this section guide you step by step through the creation of front views, 45-degree angle views and profiles. The rules vary slightly in each case, depending on whether your manga character is male or female.

Practice exercise: Male, front view

This first exercise pays particular attention to the head's basic shape when viewed from the front. The use of guidelines helps you to place facial features, such as the jaw and nose, with great accuracy. Although a head's size and shape may change, the proportionate relation between each of the features will remain the same. Typically, a male head will be larger and more angular than a female one, with a more pronounced jawline and a wider neck. Eyebrows and nose will also be thicker and more apparent.

Materials
* *cartridge paper*
* *soft lead pencil*
* *blue pencil 10*
* *pen and ink*
* *colour of your choice*

1 Begin by drawing a circle. Divide the sketch with a dotted vertical line that extends below the circle. Press lightly as you will erase these lines later (you could use a blue pencil as scanning or photocopying your finished pencil lines will eliminate the blue lines). For the jawline, draw two vertical lines extending from the left and right sides of the circle downwards, angling the lines in towards the central guide line. Join the angled lines with a small horizonal line at the very tip of the jaw. Add the shape of the neck and the start of the shoulders.

2 The size of the ears on a face defines all of the other facial characteristics. Divide the head in half with a horizontal dotted line – aligned to both the eyeline and the top of the ears. Divide the bottom half of the head in half again. This second line is the bottom of the ears and the tip of the nose. Draw the eyes and eyebrows, which are spaced equally either side of the nose and centrally with the lips. You should keep a full eye's width between them. Eyebrows almost touch the eyes at the corners when in 'neutral'.

3 The lower lip is half the distance between the tip of the nose and the chin, and is defined with simple, unfussy lines. The hairline begins halfway up the forehead, 'squaring off' the head with an off-centre parting. Keep hair choppy and natural to avoid your characters looking as if they are wearing swimming caps or strange helmets. You may wish to define cheek and collarbones. Ink your pencil lines when you are happy with them and define shadow areas.

4 Finish the head by using a colouring method of your choice. The colour stage builds on the detail and shading previously introduced. Note this example creates a unique manga colour scheme of prematurely white hair and bright green eyes to give a striking effect. Try creating your own variations on this simple formula: it's easy to create new looks just by varying the size of the various facial components.

Practice exercise: Female, front view

Female manga faces have a softer feel, which is particularly apparent in the front view. They are less angular and are usually smaller than their male counterparts, with more smoothly integrated features, particularly along the jawline. The basic design rules are the same as for the male head, but are adapted for a more feminine look, especially with regard to the eyes, which are wider, with more fully defined lashes, and the smaller, button nose.

Materials

- *cartridge paper*
- *soft lead pencil*
- *blue pencil 10*
- *pen and ink*
- *colour of your choice*

1 As for the male face, draw a circle with a vertical line through its centre. Create the jawline; this time the lines coming from the circle should be shorter, and angled slightly inwards. Keep the jawline smooth, and more rounded compared to the male.

2 Add the other guidelines, starting with the eye and nose. The proportions between each part are just the same as on the male face, but the features are different: draw eyes larger and more widely spaced, the nose smaller, and the eyebrows arch up and out.

3 Female characters tend to have longer hair, though it begins at the same hairline, even if it sweeps down and across, as in this example. Define your pencil lines by inking those you are happy with. Pay attention to the clump of eyelashes and the light glares on each eye.

4 The colour stage pulls the drawing together, with the purples of the girl's clothing reflected in her skin tone, hair and eyes. Note that female lips are defined through colour, rather than line work. Focus special attention on the colour strokes in the hair.

Male and female characteristics

Manga often uses androgynous-looking characters and outlandish hairstyles so it can be worth focusing on the major differences between the sexes: comparative sizes of eyes, noses and mouths.

Defined differences ▶
Although the male and female characters have similar jawlines and long hair, it is easy to spot the differences between them. The boy (top) has a wide, neutrally shaded mouth, compact eyes and a nose defined with a vertical line. The girl (right) has large, lashed eyes, nostrils rather than a nose, and a mouth shaded in pink.

Axes of symmetry and perspective

Simple guidelines keep features in proportion to one another while the guides are rotated in perspective. The vertical axis divides the face lengthwise and shows the angle of the head. The horizontal axis indicates whether the face is looking up or down.

▶ Three-quarter perspective looking down

▶ Three-quarter perspective looking down (from higher up)

▶ Three-quarter perspective looking up

Practice exercise: Male face, 45-degree angle view

In this exercise, the male head is drawn at a 45-degree angle, which gives more depth to his features, such as the chin and cheekbones. Here, the character is looking towards his left.

Materials
- *cartridge paper*
- *soft lead pencil*
- *blue pencil 10*
- *pen and ink*
- *colour of your choice*

1 Start with a solid circle but add a convex vertical dotted line to show where the centre of the face will point. Extend a solid curved line down from the lower half of the head and back to the base of the ears, forming a slanted angle for the chin.

2 Draw the pencil guides for the eyes, ears, eyebrows and the mouth as before: half the head height for the eyeline, half of the remaining space for the noseline. Ink in the outlines of the eyes, eyebrows nose and mouth.

3 Complete the detail of the eyes and the rest of the features of the face. Note how the right eyebrow and nose form a reverse 'S' shape. Draw in your hair as before, showing the back of the head behind the ear and extended fringe.

4 Finish the head by adding colour, noting areas of shadow. Shading on the skin reveals the form of the face – note the shadows beneath the cheekbones, on the neck, under the lips and nose and beneath the hair and eyebrows.

Practice exercise: Female face, 45-degree angle view

In this exercise, a female head is drawn at a 45-degree angle. Again, the character is looking left, towards us. The female head has a shorter jawline, a more triangular chin and more delicate features than the male face.

Materials
- *cartridge paper*
- *soft lead pencil*
- *blue pencil 10*
- *pen and ink*
- *colour of your choice*

1 Start with a solid circle and a convex, extended dotted vertical pencil line. Extend a solid curved line down from the lower half of the head and back to the base of the ears, forming the slanted angle of the chin. Note the smoother, shallower jawline and thinner neck.

2 Draw the pencil guides for the eyes, ears, eyebrows and the mouth as before: half the head height for the eyeline, half of the remaining space for the noseline. Ink in the outlines of the eyes, eyebrows nose and mouth. Don't connect the brow with the nose.

3 Build up your detail in ink. The ear is smaller than the male, the neck begins farther back from the chin and the nose is more refined. Eyebrows are farther from the nose. Eyelashes protrude outside the head silhouette on the far side. Pay attention to the neat hairline.

4 Colour defines the shape of the head: here a 'V' of lit areas, with shade under the nose, eyes and mouth. Highlights on the forehead, cheeks and under the tip of the nose add dimensionality and life to the skin.

Practice exercise: Male face, profile view

Earlier, we saw how the facial guidelines can be rotated in any direction. While faces in profile use this same structure, the features can often look very different, with the eyes, nose and mouth taking on new shapes, as seen below.

Materials
- *cartridge paper*
- *soft lead pencil*
- *blue pencil 10*
- *pen and ink*
- *colour of your choice*

1 Draw guides for the basic circle of the face, adding a pointed jaw to create a 'plectrum' shape. This represents the front of the face below the nose, with the curve under the circle becoming the jawline. Draw guides for the neck.

2 Draw in dotted horizontal guide lines to define the eyes, ears and mouth. Viewed from the side, eyes become a curved 'V' shape, as does the nose. Note how the upper lip protrudes over the lower lip. Eyebrows curve in towards the nose.

3 Ink your sketched-in features. Add hair, remembering that the hairline may be covered from the side, and that the hair extends back in a squared-off fashion. Ink your pencil lines. Add shading for the cheek-bones and glare on the eyes.

4 Colour gives 'weight' to the image, with the back of the head covered in shadow. The sharp-angled silhouette presents more defined features than a front view, so profile shots can rely less on colour to differentiate features from one another.

Practice exercise: Female face, profile view

Here we see a female head, drawn in the same direction as the male, and using exactly the same basic building blocks and guidelines. Note the lips are far fuller in profile, the nose more rounded, and the brow emphasized far less.

Materials
- *cartridge paper*
- *soft lead pencil*
- *blue pencil 10*
- *pen and ink*
- *colour of your choice*

1 Start just as you did for the male profile. Keep the jawline shallower and the neck more slender. While the male jawline juts down from the ear, the female jaw swoops towards the chin in a gentle curve.

2 Add in your horizontal dotted guidelines, and features such as ears and nose. Start to ink in the eyes and mouth. Note that the female lips are fuller and more defined, with the chin not jutting out as far.

3 Ink in the nose, jaw and eye, remembering that the female eye is larger and sweeps back farther. Allow space above the eye for a smooth eyebrow arch that starts just above the front of the iris.

4 Complete the girl's profile by colouring the head, paying particular attention to the eyes, lips and highlights in the hair. Check for areas of highlight noting that half of the face and all of the neck is in shadow.

Drawing eyes

Eyes are extremely versatile, and have a marked effect on the facial expression of any character, determining gender, age, and also emotional state. Our eyes are perhaps the most expressive part of our faces, and often reveal emotions that we are attempting to hide. You can cover up all of a character's other features and show how they are reacting solely with the eyes. Not surprising, then, that the eyes are one of the trickier parts of the body to get right, as you need to learn how to express moods as well as get to grips with basic eye anatomy. To express shock or surprise, for example, you should raise the top eyelids high above the pupils. For a cool look, cut them midway across. Although manga faces are filled with a liquid shine to make them seem more emotional, most have little tone, which is why it is important to get as much expression out of their features as you can.

The eyebrows act as 'backup' to the eyes. They work in a similar way to bars on a gate: raised eyebrows seem open and friendly, lowered eyebrows appear closed and unfriendly. One eyebrow up and one down conveys doubt. Level eyebrows suggest a character who is non-committal. Following similar principles, animals such as cats and dogs often express themselves with a tilt of the head and movement of the ears.

Eyes

There are exceptions, but many manga characters have large eyes. The eyes are said to be windows to the soul, and because the Japanese are obsessed with mood and emotion, their readers expect to look right inside. The more they see, the greater the empathy they experience with the character. To Western readers, the big-eye look can be deceptive. Characters that appear to be little kids could, in fact, be fully grown adults; they may look cute, but their behaviour does not reflect this. This misunderstanding has caused issues of censorship in the West, where comics are perceived to be for children.

> **Tip:** Eyes that reflect light look more animated and human than those without. See for yourself how removing the highlights and subtle reflections makes a character's eyes look dull and doll-like.

Huge irises and large pupils are common in the female characters.

Narrower eyes with cropped irises and small pupils are common in male characters.

Female eyes ▲

As female eyes are large, there is ample opportunity to make a feature of the play of light across the pupil (the black centre) and iris (the coloured surrounding area). The eyebrows of female characters are thin, and the eyelashes prominent.

Male eyes ▲

The eyes of male characters tend to be thinner and narrower than female eyes, although there are a few exceptions. Eyebrows are thicker, with no eyelashes. Male characters have light glares in their eyes, too, although not as large or obvious.

◀ **Jagged eyebrow**
Often used in manga to help exaggerate more suspicious, villainous characteristics, jagged eyebrows and eyelashes (in female characters) are used for big or exceptional personalities.

◀ **Streamlined eyebrow**
This is the most commonly drawn eyebrow shape. It can be straight, arched, a 'hill', or a subtle top of a 'wave' (like this one).

Practice exercise: Standard female big eye

There are many ways to draw eyes, starting either with a basic circle or the upper eyelid. Using a 'V' shape as a guide is probably the easiest method for beginners.

1 Draw a tall 'V' as a guide and add two opposing arcs between the two lines. Ink in the eyelids, which arc out then slope in towards the white of the eye.

2 Add a central oval for the pupil and a larger oval to create the iris and lights in the cornea. Add a thin eyebrow and place above the eye.

3 Finally, add eyelashes. When viewed from the front like this, they should point mainly to the side. Colour the eye.

Practice exercise: Standard male eye

Male eyes are thinner than female eyes. The eye drawn here is a fairly standard size. If it were drawn much thinner, the character would look like a villain.

1 The V-shaped guides can be used, but this time spread them wider apart. Ink in a slightly slanted curve, with the left side curving in slightly. Next draw the curve of the bottom eyelid.

2 The iris of the male eye is circular, held within the confines of the eyelids. Start by pencilling a perfect circle through the eye, then ink over the parts of the circle that remain within the eyelids.

3 Add a couple of areas of white on the iris to show light bouncing off the cornea. Then add the eyebrow, which should be thicker than the female version. Colour the eye.

Practice exercise: Female villain eye

A female villain should look threatening and devious. You can achieve this simply by making the eye much narrower than the standard female big eye shown above.

1 If using the 'V', the lines should be farther apart at the top than before. The farther apart the lines, the narrower the eye. Draw a curved slant, with the left edge (nearest the nose) lower than the other.

2 Add the iris: again you can draw an entire circle in the centre of the eye, making sure your circle goes outside the eyelids. For a calculating squint, add an extra short arch between the eyebrow and the eye, up to half the width of the eye.

3 Add subtle light reflections. When shading, make sure the iris isn't black, so the pupil stands out. Add fewer eyelashes than before. The top of the eyebrow should be jagged.

Practice exercise: Male villain eye

The eye of a male villain is very similar to that of a female villain. The differences between the two amount to tweaks.

1 Ink in a curved slant, with the left edge lower than the other. Add the iris, cropped within the confines of the eyelid. Add subtle light reflections.

2 The eyebrow is sleek like the female's, but slightly thicker, and more angular and jagged. Add the extra line to imply the squint, but make it longer for the male villain.

3 The lower part of the eye is more triangular than the upper lid. Instead of lower eyelashes, add a thick line of shadow. Colour the eye.

Drawing hair

Hair can be difficult to get right, and it helps to break styles into separate components. The hairstyle in question, like other personal characteristics in manga, will be affected by genre. Individual strands are implied by the few that are drawn into the different-sized bunches, tufts or clumps.

As with clothes, fashionable or outlandish haircuts are the norm, so keep yourself appraised of the latest trends – or start some of your own. Manga in black and white means your characters need to have unique silhouettes that read well without colour, and hair plays a major part in this.

How hair sits on the scalp

Manga hair can be divided into two main styles: hair that grows up and out from the scalp, and hair that lies flat against the scalp. Once you've mastered these basic styles, you can combine the two in an infinite number of combinations to create interesting styles for more prominent characters. Start with drawing only nine or ten strands. Later, once you've got the knack of drawing basic hair, you can make it more detailed.

Tip: Remember that hair follows the shape of the scalp. When starting out, it will be helpful to draw the entire head, bald, and add hair proportionally over the outline you have drawn.

Tied-back, male ▲
Hair is pulled back and tied up at the top of the head in a rather androgynous fashion.

Shoulder-length, layered ▲
Detail is concentrated in the strands around the face, leaving the top of the hair to glossily reflect the light.

Spiked and styled ▲
This gravity-defying cut is made of a number of spiked strands. Block in the main shape of the hair first, then add spikes as appropriate. Note that, while intricate, not every strand of hair has been drawn. Hair frames the face.

Tresses ▲
Coils of long hair suggest a pampered princess – whether from the Dark Ages or California.

Swept ▲
Perfect for the model student with a 'dark' side. Choppily cut short, with the hair swept to one side.

Drawing a fringe, or 'bangs'

A fringe (bangs) – the term used for hair that either entirely or partially covers the forehead – are often referred to in the process of manga creation. They form one of the essential building blocks of hairstyles. Creating a fringe is not unlike designing a helmet. Once you've sketched the frame, craft the hair over the top. Make the fringe consistent, but not even – you don't want to give your character a 'bowl cut' (unless this is appropriate to your character). Let a few strands go astray to make the hairstyle more realistic.

For a fringe, draw hair down over the forehead towards the eyes and bridge of the nose. The arc of the hair should go back up towards the top centre of the head, giving the illusion the fringe is following the front curve of the head. On the left side, arcs curve up to the right, and on the right side, to the left. An arc will curve less towards the middle of the fringe.

A fringe to the front of the head ▶
A blunt-cut fringe is complemented by chunky hair to the sides of the face.

A fringe to the front of the head ▲
A fringe swept to the side to reveal the forehead.

A long fringe to the front of the head ▲
A choppy, uneven fringe obscures the eyes.

A short fringe to the front of the head ▲
Blunt-cut fringe and puffed-out hair add interest.

A long fringe to the side of the head ▲
A simple inverse-'V' shape, parted on the right.

Adding curves to hair

Get into the habit of curving your hair strands. The longer your character's hair, the longer the curves should be.

Curves on shorter hair ▲
Note how the coils are layered over one another, suggesting depth and making the hair look natural.

Big curvy or wavy hair ▲
Here, the curves emanate from a central point at the back of the head, growing narrower as they progress.

Curves on long, straight hair ▲
Less layers, but more pronounced curves as the strands reach their tips.

Tip: Make sure that the characteristics are easily distinguished in black and white, as most manga is not printed in colour. Remember that there's no need for consistency if one of the hairstyles is changed by magic.

Drawing the mouth and nose

In manga, the mouth and nose are probably the simplest areas of the face to draw, and some of the standard methods can be used interchangeably for either gender. In some forms of manga, a relatively realistic nose is acceptable, although generally only for the male characters. Female noses, whatever the genre, tend to be drawn minimally.

Simple noses

The simplest noses comprise a pair of curves in profile. The first line starts at the bridge of the nose and curves both downwards and outwards. The end of the line should be gently upturned, but more blunt than pointed. The second starts where the first ends, and curves slightly downwards, back towards the face. Keep the nose small, without nostrils, and the lines thin. Thick lines draw too much attention, and the nose shouldn't distract from the rest of the face.

Adding shadow and detail

You can enhance simple noses by using shadows, thickening lines with subtle shadow towards the nose's point. Shape the shadow like a black arrowhead, as if the nose is lit from above and to one side.

Adding nostrils, as shown below, can also add interest and dimensionality. A hooked horizontal line for the nasal aperture is usually enough: you don't need to draw the 'hoods' of skin on either side of the main stem of the nose.

Female   Female   Female

Male   Male   Male

Male nose ▲
These two pictures show just how subtle the differences between the sexes are. The male nose is longer and more 'snubbed' at the tip.

Female nose ▲
On the other hand, the curve of this nose is smaller and tilted upwards. The focus is on the tip of the nose, rather than suggesting the nostrils.

shadow, from side, nostril   shadow, from side, no nostril   shadow, from front, side-lit

strongly side-lit, nostril   top-lit shadow   from front, side-lit, nostril

◀ **Shading in colour**
Using a darker skin tone underneath the nostrils allows you to keep the minimalist detail and inking of an unshadowed nose while still adding a degree of dimensionality.

Tip: Noses on the male face tend to have more definition and detail than the smaller female nose, which also has a more rounded end. Some forms abandon the nose entirely on the female face.

Drawing mouths

Like the nose, the mouth is kept simple in manga. Often, a thin line is enough to suggest it (when closed, at least), though the mouths of women and girls are often fully rendered in colour. In almost all cases, mouths are small, unless the character is yelling, screaming or laughing heartily.

When you draw a character that is looking anywhere other than straight ahead, you will need to consider the curve of the nose and mouth – the lower lip should curve outwards, down towards the chin, and the upper lip inwards, up towards the nose. Both follow the curves of the face.

> **Tip:** When a character is shouting, it's the jaw that does the majority of the moving and heavy emotional lifting, so focus your attention on the lower lip.

Simple female angled ▲
Dots mark the corners, a curve hints at a smile.

Simple female straight ▲
A triangle of shade under the line gives definition to lips.

Simple male angled ▲
A simple line serves as well for men as for women.

Simple male straight ▲
There's little to differentiate the sexes from the front.

Complex female angled ▲
Lines show the 'plumpness', colour does the rest.

Complex female straight ▲
Note the more realistic line showing where the lips meet.

Complex male angled ▲
Lips are thinner and shaded in standard flesh tone.

Complex male straight ▲
Look out for the shallow 'U' underneath the mouth.

Practice exercise: Building the female mouth

Female mouths in manga are more fully rendered than their male equivalents, with more-defined lips and colour rendering.

Materials
- *cartridge paper*
- *soft lead pencil*
- *blue pencil 10*
- *pen and ink*
- *colour of your choice*

1 Draw the outlines of a head in the usual way, drawing in guides for the eyes, nose, and mouth. The mouth sits at the base of the guide circle, where it connects to the jaw.

2 Start with the open aperture of the mouth, adding a small 'dip' above suggesting the groove that joins the nose to the mouth, and a curve beneath for the bottom lip.

3 Fill out the lip lines as shown above. Tilt the mouth aperture inwards so that the open mouth forms 'V' shapes on either side, and add 'dimples'. Don't connect the lines of the lips; instead, fill the shape with colour.

> **Tip:** If you want to keep the proportions and position of the mouth you've drawn, but give it fuller lips, thicken the inked outline around the mouth.

Facial expressions

A person's face can display a large range of emotions, delivered to the rest of the world through changes in expression. These different expressions are used in comics to evoke the inner feelings and thoughts of a character, often making dialogue unnecessary. Your audience should be able to read a character's angry expression, for example, without the artist having to add 'I'm angry!' in a speech balloon or caption. Expression can be seen as a wordless form of communication and is one of the most important tools used in drawing any comic strip. On a technical level, emotions are represented by altering the looks of the mouth and eyes, making them work in concert. In some cases – particularly when creating mysterious or villainous manga characters – you may want to leave the true emotions of your character in question, in which case concealing either the eyes or mouth of that character will increase the ambiguity surrounding them.

Adapting each expression

As you work through the following techniques, you will soon discover how it is easier to draw a new expression then adapt it from another. The key is in the little things, and making small changes. Sometimes all it takes is a subtle alteration to the mouth or the arch of the brow to completely change a character's mood. If you want to practise simpler forms of expression, you can use a pair of dots for eyes, a single line for the nose, a pair of lines for eyebrows, and a mouth that varies from a straight line to a curved shape, depending on the character's mood.

Neutral happy ▲
Slightly raised eyebrows create an open but neutral expression.

Pleased ▲
The corners of the mouth tilt up in a smile, the eyebrows begin to raise.

Pleasantly surprised ▲
The eyebrows shoot up and the smile becomes more obvious.

Delighted ▲
The eyes close, the smile is a full 'U' curve, the eyebrows vanish in the hairline.

Neutral sad ▲
Flat eyebrows add a sad tinge to this neutral expression.

Glum ▲
Eyebrows begin to lift next to the nose, while the mouth dips at either side.

Broken ▲
The eyebrow slope deepens, the corners of the mouth head towards the chin.

Distraught ▲
The mouth is an inverted 'U', the eyebrows an open bascule bridge.

Neutral angry ▲
The slight curve of the mouth suggests something has irked this character.

Grumpy ▲
The brows furrow and the curve of the mouth becomes more pronounced.

Irate ▲
Eyebrows thicken and teeth become visible as inner tensions start to spill out.

Furious ▲
Brows nearly meet in the middle, the mouth twists down, with teeth visible.

Seven facial expressions

Here are some common expressions. You can vary these – nothing is set in stone – so if another way of conveying anger or happiness occurs to you, try it out. You can also look in the mirror, or take photographs of friends mimicking these emotions, to give yourself a better idea of the various shapes and lines made naturally by the face.

Annoyed ▲
Keep the pupils small to show your character's displeasure. The closed mouth is drawn as an arch, and should look sullen and petulant. Eyebrows indicate a vexed expression.

Friendly ▲
The eyebrows form subtle arches. A thin line above the eyelashes indicates the eyelids are relaxed. The face shows interest and openess. The eyes are wide open and the mouth is smiling.

Angry ▲
Shape the eyebrows so that the corners nearest the nose point straight down, and rise steeply on to the forehead. Reduce the size of the pupils to a tiny dot, or leave them out altogether. Some artists further convey rage by fanging the teeth.

Happy ▲
These eyebrows are high arches, the eyes similarly closed to evoke elation. The mouth is much bigger than the 'friendly' mouth, drawn as a blunt upturned triangle. The left and right corners of the mouth are turned upwards.

Sad
The features in this expression are a combination of surprise and upset. The mouth is small, the eyes wide open and crying. The eyebrows are narrow 'S' shapes lying on their sides. Above the eyes, an extra arch gives the lids a touch more emphasis. This character is openly crying but you can show the anticipation of tears with extra patches of reflected light, and by giving the iris and pupil fuzzy edges to suggest extra moisture in the eyes. If you want the tears to be more apparent, add a couple of cloud-shapes in the corners of the eyes. You can also draw a couple of extra upward slants under the inner side of the eyebrows to show the raising of the forehead.

Evil ▲
The eyebrows are thin, pointy and more angular than angry ones. The eyes are angled downwards. Make the eyelids, pupils and lashes thick and dark; shrouded and sinister. The nose is pointy, almost sharp, and the mouth needs to have a smiling or a smirking element to it: the character is enjoying himself. To suggest extreme evil, try gritted teeth and a broad smile. The smirk shown here is achieved with a straight line that is upturned at one end.

Surprise ▲
The expression on this girl's face indicates surprise and disbelief. The eyes are wide open, showing the whites of the eyes surrounding the irises. The black pupils are big, hollow circles. The mouth is rounder than 'friendly' and 'happy', and the expression of shock is indicated as an 'O' shape.

The manga figure

In any style of cartooning, whether traditional or manga, the figure takes precedence. Readers notice the human character before everything else, because it is almost always the element that carries the narrative. Human bodies come in all shapes and sizes, from little children to muscled giants, so your manga universe would be boring if everybody looked the same. As you did for the head, start by practising the basic shapes and structures of the human figure.

Constructing the body

Basic anatomical construction comes from understanding the abstract shapes of the human body, and how they act in relation to one another. Whether by studying a skeleton, or by breaking down an existing figure drawing into simple components, learn to see each segment of the figure as part of the whole. Using simple shapes like spheres, tubes and curves, you can block in the proportions of your poses and clear up any anatomical mistakes before you add in the detail work. Pay attention to where limbs connect, and how different parts of the body alter with perspective.

◀ **Simplified anatomy**
Before working up to a high degree of detail on your characters, it can often be helpful to block out the shape of each pose using simplified structures like these. Focus on getting the correct lengths of each limb and the appropriate attitude and rotation of each joint.

◀ **The layout stage**
Boil down each pose to its essential components. Pay attention to the waist and hips as they twist away from the default pose. Use the head's 'crosshairs' to show where a character is looking. Don't forget that photo reference can often prove invaluable.

Tip: Manga heroes are slim and attractive, so keep them toned, not bulky. If you want to show physical strength, increase the muscle mass around the thighs, the shoulders, the chest and the arms. Don't exaggerate to the extent that you create a 'superheroic' inverse-'V' shape, i.e. a torso larger than the legs can realistically support.

Gender differences ▲
The ribcage that defines the chest is broader on the male than the female, but female hips are wider in proportion to the chest than male hips. In these simplified skeletons, oval shapes are used for the skull, chest and hips. Male versions are more angular.

Manga musculature

Male and female characters in manga are often more developed than someone of their age would normally be. Once you've got used to drawing proportional outlines, you can add the muscle, skin and detailing that create the finished outline of your character.

Tip: You can vary a character's amount of muscle by varying the distance from the bones at which you flesh them out. Muscle is shown sparingly on female figures in order to retain their slenderness.

Head and shoulders

Male manga characters have wider shoulders than female characters. Though some artists say the shoulder width of a male character should be the equivalent of three heads, your heroes will look like muscleheads if you always follow this rule. Experiment with bigger head proportions to find the best size.

Skeletal structure

It is well worth studying the human skeleton, even if you have mastered using simple shapes to lay out your figures, as it will reinforce your knowledge of basic anatomy and how every part of the body fits together.

Male body ▲
Here is the fully defined male form, with skin and musculature grafted over the simple layout shapes. Note how strongly the muscles are defined, drawing attention to the joints of the skeleton beneath.

Female body ▲
Female manga forms are far less overtly muscled than the males: joints are suggested by gentle curves, not rendering. Tissue is denser in the breasts and around the hips, creating an obviously female silhouette.

Proportion

As you go on to customize the form of your characters, they will take on their own dimensions. Their proportions – the distances between features – may become longer or shorter. You may also decide to make their overall size or the size of certain parts of the body larger or smaller. Whatever forms you develop, your characters' movements need to conform to the new proportions you define whenever they appear in order to be convincing. Then, no matter what they look like, the reader will accept their essential reality. Manga artists define the proportions of the adult body through the use of the size of the head: seven or eight times deep for a standard male or female protagonist, nine heads for an Amazon or male superhero, six or seven heads for adolescents, between five and six heads for a child, and two or three heads for super-deformed (exaggerated) characters or chibi-style (short person) characters.

Use these rules as a basis, but adjust them according to your needs. As before, make sure you are consistent: using a guide allows you to maintain character proportions throughout an entire story. There are key differences in the physique that when drawn, help readers determine whether or not the character is female or male. For a female these include narrower shoulders, a thinner waist, higher hips and less muscle definition, smaller facial features and curves.

Female body proportions

A manga artist works out a character's proportions in relation to head size. The technical term for this rule is the 'canon of proportion'. Manga females are usually petite and their proportions reflect the ideal of beauty as defined for Japanese women. Developed muscles are less aesthetic. It's common, however, to add voluptuous curves to differentiate women from girls.

◄ Pre-school female
The body of a young female is four to five heads deep. She is rounder and less defined than an adult. Notice the disproportionate roundness of her head and huge oval eyes.

> **Tip:** The rules of proportion mean that whatever the height or build of your characters, they will 'read' as human: from 1m to 100m (3ft to over 300ft tall). You can change limb lengths, but be aware that they may be construed as odd.

◄ Pre-teen female
The pre-teen female is five to six heads deep. The chubbiness has all but gone, and there is more definition in the body and face. The eyes are slightly smaller and less oval. The girl is approaching adolescence, as shown by her small bust, developing hips and slender legs.

Teenage female ►
The teenage female is six to seven heads deep. The hips and thighs have broadened since the pre-teen stage, and there is a noticeable bust. The face is more angular, the eyes smaller, and the fringe (bangs) is more pronounced. Her arms show greater muscle definition.

Adult female ▼
The average adult female stands eight heads deep and is tall and slim, while still curvaceous. Classic 'hourglass' proportions (bust and hips) produce an elegant and graceful frame.

Male body proportions

Most characters in manga are young male adults, for the simple reason that they constitute the target market. Males in general fluctuate widely between heavily musclebound types and sylphlike androgynes. Bishonen (meaning beautiful youth or boy) style, for example, reduces the male body to a graceful, slender physique with only slight indications of muscle, and a notable lack of nipples or body hair. Whether drawing males or females, it's helpful to develop a working knowledge of human physiology, so that you can appreciate the layout of muscles and bones. Start by learning how to draw realistically – you can modify the examples into your own style later.

◀ Pre-school male
Four to five heads is the recognized canon measure for young children. Aside from a disproportionately large head, the male child has chubby, undefined limbs, much like his female counterpart, and a rounder face than the teen or adult male. In manga, the younger you make a character, be it male or female, the larger their head is in relation to the rest of the body.

Tip: Consider joining a life-drawing class. Regular classes will improve your fundamental understanding of the human form. If a class isn't possible, drawing yourself in the mirror is a good starting point. Try drawing clothed figures, too, noting how the different fabrics gather and stretch over the human figure.

Pre-teen male ▶
The pre-teen male is five to six heads deep. By this age he is reasonably lithe, with slender limbs. His skeletal and muscular development doesn't yet support the strong body shape of adulthood, but his chest has broadened significantly since the pre-school years, and he has more muscle definition. Keep the shoulders of pre-teens relatively undeveloped, and keep the length of the limbs similarly constrained.

Adult male ▲
Fully grown, our male protagonist now stands seven to eight heads deep and carries himself with an upright stance. He is super fit and strong. But while the muscle tone is more defined, and his shoulders are far broader, he lacks the powerfully solid torso and exaggerated abdominals and chest pectorals of the average superhero. His chin is no longer pointy and his new, square jaw almost matches the width of his cheekbones.

Teenage male ▶
Now in his teens, the male character has increased muscle definition, particularly in the arms and shoulders, and stands between six and seven heads deep. He is still slender, and his figure is drawn with simple, sleek vertical lines and very few curves. Compared to the pre-teen male, his face is more angular, the eyes smaller, and he has a more defined fringe at the hairline.

Drawing hands

In creating expression, a character's hands are almost as important as their face. A hand gesture, like a facial expression, can convey how a character is feeling without them having to say anything. If your character is talking, but is not being sincere, then their hands can reveal their true emotion and give them away. If a character's face is not visible, but their hands are, you can easily show they are tense or angry with a clenched fist. Open palms can indicate friendship or surrender. Because the hands have numerous joints and are so flexible, there are literally hundreds of ways in which you can depict them. Start by picking a few easy positions and practise drawing these.

Practice exercise: Open hand

Open hands usually indicate a passive or relaxed person. If they are held above the head, they show the character is trying to attract help or attention. If they are held out in front of the body they may represent a plea to stop.

Materials
* cartridge paper
* soft lead pencil
* pen and ink
* colour of your choice

1 Start with an abstract shape, like the head of a broom or a mitt, beginning at the wrist and flaring upwards and outwards to create the basic hand shape of two arcs joined together.

2 At a position roughly the same length away from the hand as the size of the hand, inscribe an upper arc. Add four lines for the fingers, with the middle finger the longest. Jut out the thumb like the spout of a kettle.

3 Thicken out the finger guides, using your own hand to accurately estimate their proportions. Note where the fingers intersect with the palm and back of the hand: in the centre of this guide line is where the knuckle falls. Each finger subdivides into three sections, extending from the knuckle.

4 Draw around your guides, fleshing out the musculature and giving the hand definition. Add fingernails, as well as small upward arcs to shape the knuckle joints, using the line guides from the previous step. Ink your favoured pencil lines and add colour as necessary.

Palm of hand

Repeat the first few steps, but don't add fingernails or knuckles. Instead, add the main areas in the skin of the palm: a pair of horizontal lines across the centre, an arc across the wrist, and arcs to show where the thumb and the flesh of the hand protrude.

Hand movement

Study how the hand moves, both in the realm of individual fingers – pointing, fists, open palms – but also in how the hand relates to the arm: how it rotates and flexes around the wrist.

Gender differences

In manga tradition, a female hand is not as wide as a male one, and the fingers are longer and more delicate. A female's open palm does not show very many creases and any ones that are included are more subtle.

A range of hands ▶
Why not devote a section of your sketch pad to capturing hand poses from life or magazines? Try different shades of skin colour.

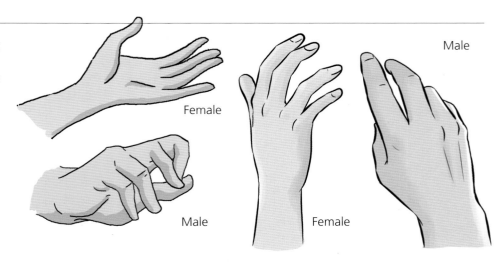

Female

Male

Male

Female

Hands at different ages

When you draw an elderly hand, add more lines around the fingers and joints. You should also make the fingers thicker and less sleek. When you draw a very young hand, keep the fingers small and underdeveloped; their length should only slightly exceed the length of the palm of the hand.

Square versus smooth ▶
Older hands are more angular than young, as joints begin to protrude through thinning skin.

Young

Old

◀ The extremes of age
The hands of young and old characters are drawn to the same proportions as their bodies: a child's hands are short and stubby because they are not yet fully grown. With faces, the rule of ageing is that every additional line adds a year to the character's life – it's a similar case for hands.

Studies of hands

It's vital that a manga artist be able to draw the hand in a wide range of positions, and you should practise as often as you can. Look at the way your own hand moves, and you'll notice its versatility: you can change the way it looks by moving just one of your five fingers (not to mention the wrist). The examples shown here show the hands in a range of positions.

Flustered hands ▲
It's all too much for this character, who takes a breather, resting her hand on her forehead. Note how her fingers interact with the hair and forehead.

◀ Holding hands
Here's a masterless samurai's hand, gripping tightly to his katana. Note how the hand interacts with an object.

Hands in perspective ▲
Here's a pose captured using a mirror or photo reference. Never forget that it's rare to see a hand in manga from the same perspective as you would see your own: experiment with angles.

Drawing feet

As well as hands, you need to think about your character's feet. Most of the time, these feet will probably be inside shoes, although it may occasionally be appropriate to draw a character barefoot. Feet are often used to convey travel within a story – a close-up panel of a character's feet will tell the reader they are approaching their destination, or else emphasize the passing of time during a journey. If you find drawing feet difficult, take comfort from the fact you are in good company. Many artists hate drawing feet, and some will go to great lengths not to show them. It can be difficult to get the feet right in relation to the rest of the figure, and it is a common mistake to draw feet too big. Start your training with a series of simple shapes as a basis, and then draw the positions of the feet within the guides. You should practise drawing both sides of the feet from various angles in order to understand as much as possible about this part of the body.

Practice exercise: Side view

It's easiest to think of a foot viewed from the side as a right-angled triangle with the longest edge as the base of the foot. These steps will allow you to flesh out that underlying shape.

Materials
- *cartridge paper*
- *blue pencil 10*
- *soft lead pencil*
- *pen and ink*
- *colouring method of your choice*

> **Tip:** Bulky, heavy characters should not be given small, perfectly formed feet, unless you are drawing attention to their mismatched proportions. Adapt the standard feet shown here by thickening up the dimensions, remembering that muscle tissue, fatty deposits and skin can increase in size, but the bones underneath do not. This leads to chunky toes, tree-trunk like ankles and so on. An ogre's feet should be as large and ugly as his body.

1 Start with a smoothed right-angle triangle for the foot, with a rectangle on top for the leg. Add a small squashed oval to locate the big toe.

2 The inner foot should arch upwards slightly, off the ground, with the thick pad of the ball of the foot placed slightly behind the toes, and the heel falling just behind the line of the ankle.

3 Add in the toes. From this view only the big toe is visible. From the opposite side start with the little toe and work back to the big toe; the tips of each may be visible from the side, depending on the angle you choose. Use ink and colour to complete the side view.

Feet in motion

When your characters are in motion, the appearance of their feet, and the angle of the foot to the leg, is constantly changing. Although it isn't necessary to master every perspective, it's important to suggest this movement. Look out for visual references to keep in your sketchbook and use for your drawing practice.

Moving feet ▶
These simple poses show feet in various stages of motion. These can be adapted for walking, running or dancing sequences.

Practice exercise: Front view

A row of toes forms a natural curve, which begins at the big toe and ends at the smallest. Shoes should be drawn following this curve, with a rounded end instead of individual toes.

Materials
- *cartridge paper*
- *soft lead pencil*
- *pen and ink*
- *colour of your choice*

1 Begin with a trapezoid shape for the feet with a rectangle on top for the leg. The trapezium should be cut so it runs practically parallel with the top of the foot.

3 Add toenails, remembering to keep them blunted towards the end of the toe, and ink your favoured pencil lines. Use colour to add texture, shading and tone.

2 Subdivide the trapezium into the toes, noting the gap between the big toe and the other four. Note, too, how the feet bow outwards at the 'knuckle' of the big toe.

Tip: Draw shoes with a rough version of the foot inside for a more convincing shape. If you're still having trouble, take off your shoes, tilt them to the required angle, and sketch from life.

Toes and toenails

Each toe is a blunted rectangular shape and slightly curved. The big toe is the dominant template, each of the four other toes diminishing in a curve of size to the right or left of it, depending on the foot. Toenails end at the tip of the toe and have a rounded edge.

Ankles

The ankle is a small part of the body but necessary detail. If the foot is drawn from the side, the ankle is represented by a small arc that protrudes from the leg. The ankle is shown as two lines that slope gently outwards. The ankle joint on the outer leg should be drawn slightly lower and closer to the foot than the ankle on the inside leg.

Foot extended

Observe how the foot appears at rest, and when it bends. If you look at a foot from the side, pointed straight down, toes to the ground, you'll see that its top is almost a straight line, but that the bottom of the foot, particularly around the heel and toe, protrudes and creates a crease in the skin where it meets the top of the foot.

Shoes over toes

Drawing a completely bare foot can be difficult, and getting your character to put on shoes can make your life simpler. This way, you don't have to draw individual toes or worry about getting the heel in the correct position. It's also easier to correct a mistake when drawing a pair of shoes, because you are free to improvise, than it is to correct an anatomical error while drawing bare feet. It's also a lot easier to draw your own shoe from real life than it is to sketch from your own bare feet.

Movement and perspective

You need to keep your characters in motion. If you draw them in the same pose, panel after panel, you will quickly lose your audience's interest. Move them in a way that is appropriate, taking into consideration their psychology, motives and style. The poses you give your characters will define who they are within a story, and enable your audience to differentiate between them. Characters should always be recognizable, not only when they are standing still, fully lit and in the foreground, but also if they're drawn in the distance, in the shadows, or out of focus. A character should be recognizable by their smaller traits, so that even if the majority of a character's body is hidden, his or her gestures will make clear their identity. Don't confuse your readers: whatever your character is doing, whether they are sprinting, bending down, catching or throwing, show their actions clearly. This is equally true when a character is stationary: even while sitting down, a character will project a mood, an attitude and a point of view. The key to communicating all these different facets is to choose the ultimate expression of each pose – the moment that sits right at the heart of your chosen action.

Stages of movement

It is not always easy to choose the right moment: a pose that shows your character doing exactly what you want your audience to know they are doing.

It can be helpful to imagine your manga narrative as a film, which you can pause every few seconds and explain with subtitles. Of course, the grammar of film is often very different to that of manga, but try watching a chase scene and pressing 'pause' occasionally. You'll soon find your 'eye' for picking the right paused moments: those with the greatest dynamism and energy, even when frozen. Anatomy is your second watchword, as your audience must be able to recognize the poses you create – they must be physiologically plausible. Characters must never look like they are made of rubber – unless it's one of their mystical abilities. One of the best ways to sell movement is to integrate it with your backgrounds and secondary characters, whether it's puffs of dust from feet on tarmac, or a person being pushed aside as the hero races past.

Hitting the 'pause' button ▼
When reviewing your scene, capture the apex of each individual moment, the point when the potential energy of any action is released.

Stages of dynamism ▲
While any of these poses would work, the third, marked by the upswing in the red dotted line, is the most dynamic.

Tip: Find your definitive moments and draw them. Don't leave anything open to interpretation unless you aim to be ambiguous. If your audience misreads an action, it will muddy the story and detract from the pace.

Axes of perspective

Since manga is two-dimensional, you must find methods of implying a third, to give your characters depth. Using axes can help establish perspective, which will make your characters look more natural as they move within their environment.

The axes comprise two horizontal axes (X, across the horizon of your image; Y, into and out of the image) and a vertical axis (Z, up and down the image). These axes are rotated with respect to where the 'ground' is in the image you are drawing. Picture the vertical axis as your character's centre of gravity, and rotate limbs and poses around this anchor, thus keeping you tethered to the possible and allowing you to turn the character in 3-D space.

X, Y and Z axes ▼
The spine ascends on the Z axis. Points on his body tilt away from the 90-degree angles on the X and Y axes, giving him energy even standing still.

Action curve

Another form of assistance is the action curve, which helps you to concentrate the body into a single flowing pose. The action line flows down the centre of the spine from the head, and changes shape and length depending upon the pose, forming the single simplest embodiment of every action. When sketching out your poses, the action line should be the first element you draw, enabling you to hang your anatomy on to the most dynamic through-line. The examples below demonstrate the use of the line in the construction of poses, showing the bold action line in blue, the layout anatomy in red, and the completed image in full colour.

Punched ▲
Note how the action line describes the arc of the whole figure, not just the position of the arms or legs.

◄ **Jumping**
In this case, the line and figure are in tight agreement, showing the release of energy vertically as the character leaps upwards.

Foreshortening

This is when parts of a character's body that are 'closer' to us are drawn much larger than those farther away, exaggerating and 'shortening' focal depth for dramatic effect. An example is of a character flying or running towards us. The character's outstretched arms or head may be large in the frame, drawing our attention, but the legs and body are smaller, pushing them farther away. It can be tricky to get the hang of this technique, but striking and punchy poses are a result worth working towards. Foreshortening also has the added benefit of making the reader feel much closer to the action.

American footballer ▲
The helmet and shoulder pad burst out of the page, the footballer appearing to barrel towards our fourth-down tackle.

Flying superhero ▲
The hero vaults into the sky, his fist and arm outpacing the rest of his body.

Practice exercise: Male running

In an action-packed manga serial, you're likely to have several characters running, whether it's towards or away from danger. Here's an opportunity to take all you have learned about proportion, anatomy, detail and dynamism, and fuse them into a single image of a shonen hero sprinting to victory. When you've finished, why not try altering the angle or pose?

Materials
* *cartridge paper*
* *soft lead pencil*
* *eraser*
* *pen and ink*
* *colour of your choice*

3 Now add the basic line work of the clothes, paying attention to the folds, and the way the jacket billows out, caught by the wind whipped up by the character's passing.

1 Start by roughing in the character's proportions, using simple geometry. Use an action line to select the most dynamic moment.

2 Add detail to the face and hair next, concentrating on the character's determined expression.

4 Add the final details, from the piping and pockets on the jacket to the crinkle lines on the trousers. Using your colouring or toning medium of choice, add your final textures.

5 Use ink and colour in your preferred medium to complete the side perspective.

▲ A different perspective
Here we switch perspective to show the character, now in running gear, foreshortened, running straight towards us.

Practice exercise: Female fighting

When you've had enough of running, it's time to turn and fight. Put into practice what you've learned about the action line, about how hands can grip weaponry, and how facial expressions can sell emotions. When you've drawn this warrior leaping into battle, why not show her from a different angle?

Materials
- *cartridge paper*
- *soft lead pencil*
- *eraser*
- *pen and ink*
- *colour of your choice*

1 As before, start your illustration with the basic geometric line work, remembering how female proportions differ from male.

2 The warrior is dressed in billowing trousers and wears thick-wristed gloves, both of which significantly change her silhouette.

On the attack ▶
Here, the action line descends from the character's head to her extended back leg. Note how the hair, robe and thrown-back arm all point along it, reinforcing her leaping stride. The forward leg is elegantly pointed to make a sharp and compact silhouette.

3 Add detail to the face, hair and hands, and generate construction lines to help you draw her bare feet in sandals.

4 Complete the pencilled image by defining folds in the clothing and the toes.

5 Use ink and colour in your preferred medium to complete the front perspective.

Stance gallery

After a lot of running around and strenuous exertion, it's time for your manga creations to relax. Unfortunately, the same can't be said for your pencil. Stationary characters can say as much, if not more, as characters sprinting or engaging in swordplay, and it's vital that you are able to communicate the differences in your characters' inner states without oversized gestures or combat manoeuvres. With practice and a little thought, you should be able to place your characters in a party situation and have your readers distinguish their personality types from stance and posture alone. After all, how often do you stand with a completely straight spine and your arms pointing down by your sides? Make sure you develop casual stances for your characters, so that they don't look like soldiers when they're not on the move.

Stance

Before drawing your characters in a stance, try standing yourself. Notice how you tend to put weight on one leg when you're relaxed (you may even favour one leg over the other every time). In placing the weight on this one leg, you are raising the corresponding hip, while the leg bearing the weight will stay straight and rigid. Your waist also bends to compensate for the tilting of the hips, and straightens at the torso. Otherwise you would fall over. The human body understands instinctively how to counterbalance itself.

The position of the body comes down to the positions and angles of the feet, hips and legs, and whatever these parts of the body do, the torso follows to balance you out. So make sure you notice when standing yourself where the weight is distributed, which leg it is on, what your feet are doing (using the heel, the toes, or both) and how far apart your legs are. Try standing in front of a full-length mirror and running through the stances on this spread. See if you can improve on them, or add your own twists. Try to fill a sketchbook page with stances in simple spheres-and-tubes geometry.

Teenagers ▲
A mixture of unearned confidence and overblown angst, these teenagers manage to be cocky and emotionally closed at one and the same time.

Nervous ▲
This character keeps her body language locked down as she looks off, waiting for somebody or something she dreads.

Achievement/polite surprise ▲
Our chef is pleased to display the result of his experiments, while the pink-haired girl was not expecting a cake, but will accept it anyway.

◄ **Innocent**
These three girls, made up for a party, have open, unassuming body language. The kinked knees and feet pointing towards each other make for a stereotypically demure gesture. The cut of the clothes and bright fabrics are all about showing off, but without a heavily sexualized edge.

Tip: As a simple rule of body language, the farther a limb is moved away from the vertical axis – the wider spaced the legs or arms – the more outgoing the character.

◄ **Innocent student**
The glasses, dipped head, concealing fabrics, fluffy slippers and tightly clasped library books point towards another thrilling night of revising for finals.

◄ **Shy**
Arms clasped behind the back, knees pressed together and head cocked askance all speak of a character not confident in her own abilities.

Cocky ▲
If the hip-skimming clothing or naughty winks weren't enough to tip you off, the raised hip and pointing fingers speak of characters powerfully assured of their own attributes and ultimate, inevitable success.

Colouring your drawing with markers

Markers are a versatile method of colouring your illustrations. They come in a range of bold colours that reproduce well, and can be mixed and blended on the page, whether by layering using the same pen, or with darker, complementary tones. As well as producing fast-drying, naturalistic results on finished pieces, markers are also excellent for sketching and testing out colour schemes before proceeding to digital colour. Remember, for the best results, ink your drawings with Indian ink or a waterproof fineliner so that the colour and black lines don't bleed into one another. The project on this spread will walk you through the steps of colouring a young shojo heroine in a kimono using a limited palette of markers.

Practice exercise: Shojo heroine

This vivacious shojo heroine mixes cosplay (dressing in elaborate costume) with a more conservative streak in the traditional kimono and submissive posture. Perhaps she is undercover in some capacity? The illustration uses only a handful of marker colours that nonetheless create a fully rendered 3-D effect.

Materials
* cartridge paper
* soft lead pencil
* blue pencil 10
* pen and ink
* selection of manga markers (greens, pinks, purples, yellows, browns)

1 Open the illustration with a rough pencil sketch, blocking in the anatomy and basic shapes of the girl. Press lightly with the pencil so as to leave the paper as unmarked as possible. You may find it easier to draw a stick figure to help place all of the limbs before you draw the kimono over the top.

2 Work up the areas of detail in the hair and face, keeping the lines and folds on the kimono and sleeves fairly smooth. When you are happy with your pencil lines, ink them and, when dry, erase the lines as best you can.

3 Choose your first marker, picking a skin-tone shade to colour in the face and hands. Marker colouring works best if you leave highlighted areas as white, so imagine you are shining a bright light against your chosen surface. Don't colour the areas where the light is heavily concentrated; instead, colour the shadowed areas: underneath the eyes and fringe (bangs).

4 Using a darker shade of peach-brown, deepen some of the shadows on the face – concentrate these second shadows underneath the fringe and on the neck. Using purples and pinks, detail the eyes and lips. Keep the lips thin around the inked mouth, and leave a white highlight on the eye.

5 Leaving a large area of highlighted white striking the top of the girl's hair, colour in the first wave of green. Keep the green tone organic and natural by stroking over various areas of the hair a second or third time to make them darker and richer.

6 As with the skin tone, pick a darker version of the main hair colour and use it to pick out areas – or strands – of deeper shadow. For hair, use quick, individual flicks to give it body and life.

7 Switch your focus to the kimono. As the fabric is less reflective than either the hair or skin, there are fewer white highlights to worry about. Instead, build up tone in layers, colouring over the main body of colour multiple times, narrowing your area of shading each time.

8 Using a darker pink, add in harsh shadows on the right-hand side of the kimono and in the sleeves. Use golden yellow and brown markers to add detail to the belt and sandals. Detail and minimal shade is added to the towel with a grey marker. Build up the texture by stippling large, smudged dots.

Character archetypes

Most manga characters are young adults, because this is their target age group. If this is your audience, you want to make it easy for them to identify with your story. Each manga genre, from shonen to shojo and all points in between, has its own favourite character types. The clothes your characters wear, for example, will be dictated by genre, and that genre will encompass hundreds of books, each with their own leading character. How will your protagonist differ? Do they have an unusual magical power? Is he or she skilled in a particular martial art? No matter how adept, your characters may also be socially awkward – perhaps shy around members of the opposite sex, or just people in general. They might lose their temper easily, or get horribly clumsy when they are nervous. It's up to you.

Characters aimed at boys and girls

Shonen (comics for boys up to 18) and shojo (comics for girls up to 18) are both aimed at a typical teenage audience, and feature stories in which the protagonist overcomes obstacles in order to achieve an eventual goal. This type of story is known as *doryoku yuujou shouri* in Japan, which translates as 'effort friendship triumph'. The protagonist, through the obstacles overcome, also achieves improvements in him or herself, sometimes physical, sometimes mental, and sometimes bordering on the supernatural.

The characters involved in these stories usually have to use martial arts, sports, or games to progress and it is the improvement in these areas that will help them achieve their final goal. The setting for these stories varies wildly, from present day to science fiction and fantasy, or an original amalgam of all three.

Shojo heroine ▲
As shojo often deals with the interior world of emotions, this schoolgirl could be suffering a terrible crush, or be ready to deal out magical justice at just a moment's notice.

Fantasy shonen hero ▲
Sword in hand, this hero quests for the freedom of his people, and to rescue his kidnapped love.

Male protagonist

In shonen, the male protagonist must be the pivot around which the rest of the story revolves. He must achieve a great, monumental task, overcoming smaller quests and problems along the way. He is motivated in his task by friends or family, an authority figure whom he trusts (a teacher, respected elder statesman or a commanding officer), or by the actions of his villainous antagonist.

The lead character's attributes are always positive, as he is working towards the greater good. He is usually charismatic, driven by a desire for self-improvement, and physically attractive. However unique his characteristics and appearance, he will be instantly recognizable as the lead character.

Magic-wielding shonen hero ▲
Gifted by a magical talisman he found in a Kyoto junkshop, this straight-A high school student has an alternative career as a hunter of the forces of evil. When not brushing up on his grades or valedictorian speeches, he heads into the underworld in search of rogue demon half-breeds.

Female character

The main character in shojo is always female, but female leads also appear in shonen. In shonen, the female lead often displays an equal degree of strength, skill and intelligence as the male protagonist.

Generally speaking, female manga characters are attractive, young adults or adolescents who possess an air of either mystery or mischief.

◀ **Strong female lead**
More experienced than the protagonist, she gleefully humbles him at every opportunity.

Heroic character

The hero is typically a character at the peak of his or her abilities. Manga tends to make the hero a secondary character, rarely the protagonist. The hero is often a role model for the protagonist, and since the reader is identifying with the protagonist, also a role model for them. These heroic types may be either true heroes or villains, but they have abilities beyond the lead's, including strength, courage, bravery, and meta-human or mythical powers.

Hero of song and story ▲
He has roamed the land since time immemorial, putting his mythical sword to evil-doers for centuries.

Child character

Children provide a softer edge to a manga story, getting into humorous trouble because they lack the experience to do the right thing. In kodomo manga, children take the lead, often forming a team with older and more powerful allies on the strength of their charisma and wit. These allies make up for the children's lack of power, and will usually assist them in achieving their goals, or taking on a villain too strong for the kids to defeat by themselves.

Precocious child ▶
Stubborn, strong-willed and independent, this girl is always willing to strike out on her own in search of fun and adventure. Note her impish smile and wink indicate an extroverted personality.

Secondary character

Secondary characters have the potential to be protagonists, but are typically a close friend who helps stop the lead from becoming self-indulgent in his personal quest. If younger than the lead, they will have a similar effect to a child character in softening the lead's hard emotional edges.

Sometimes the secondary character is a Trojan horse, possessing an ability or skill lying dormant within them that makes them a key figure in the conclusion of the tale. A secondary character can gain an importance that is sometimes superior to that of the protagonist.

The best friend ▶
Checking his watch and looking out for hall monitors, this high schooler awaits his friend's return from a dark mirror dimension.

Super-deformed characters

Characters that are super-deformed (or SDs, as they are more commonly known) are examples of a specific style of manga caricature. The characters are typically small with stubby limbs and oversized heads, so that they resemble small children. Amateur manga artists sometimes start by drawing characters in this style because they are easier to construct. In commercial manga, this drawing style, with even greater degrees of exaggeration, is often interjected into the usual style to show a regular character's extreme emotion, such as anger or surprise, heightened to a level that would look bizarre on a more realistic manga face. When used in this way, they are known as chibi.

Super-deformed characters are meant to be cute and are often used in humorous diversions from the storyline. They also appear in shonen and seinen, which are relatively serious genres. Shirow Masamune's *Appleseed* series is a good example of this. The tales in the *Appleseed* canon are all cyberpunk thrillers and told fairly straight, but every now and then, Shirow throws in the odd bit of slapstick with a panel or two containing miniaturized versions of his characters, to define a moment of silly humour or overblown frustration.

Super-deformed characters can also be used for an entire story. These stories are always comedies, and are often tongue-in-cheek parodies of established manga genres.

Understanding body proportions

Super-deformed characters are drawn with an oversized head, hands and feet, and a small body. They can vary in height. The head is usually between a third and a half of the character's height. Generally speaking, the rule is that the smaller and more distorted the character is, the more detail you lose. Limbs and clothes are reduced to the minimum number of lines possible, and as a result, the smaller details such as elbows, knees, and other such joints are eliminated. In the case of extreme super-deformed characters, when the ratio of head to body reaches 1:1, the limbs and the torso are drawn much chubbier in order to keep everything looking connected.

> **Tip:** A good approach to the super-deformed style is to draw everything below the neck in proportion first, then crown off your character with an absurdly large head. The simpler you make the features, the funnier the super-deform moment.

Even if your character usually has a complex hair arrangement, reduce it to a few bunches or strands.

Arms should be one head length, so that if they were raised, they would only reach as far as the top of the head.

Regardless of the character's age, super-deformed heads are large, childlike and simplified to a minimum.

Eyes are always drawn big, and the mouth small. The nose is more often than not omitted.

The neck is only hinted at, or often left out completely.

Keep detail to a minimum, with only a few significant folds in clothing, for example.

Altering proportions ▲ ▶
Above is a young girl with the 'normal' proportions described earlier. By exaggerating and altering them, you can turn her into the super-deformed character shown at right.

You don't need to show anatomical detail like muscle tone, so keep the clothes and footwear looking large on the character.

Practice exercise: Creating a super-deformed character

While super-deformed characters are very simple to draw, that doesn't mean that they lack structural underpinnings. As the head is the most characteristic feature and so large in relation to the rest of the body, you should ensure you pay it the most attention. The rest of the features are simplified as much as possible.

1 Draw a circle, forming the basis of the head. Now, draw two lines across the centre of the circle to form a 'crosshair' – like on a gunsight – that divides the circle into quarters. The horizontal line is your guide for the centre of the eyes. On the lower half of the circle, define the jaw and chin a little, but keep the shape relatively round. Take the jawline to just above the horizontal line of your crosshair.

Materials
- *cartridge paper*
- *soft lead pencil*
- *pen and ink*
- *colours of your choice*

2 Draw in the eyes: the two corners of the upper eyelid should fall on your horizontal guideline. The arch of the eyebrows shows happiness. The eyes of super-deformed characters do not contain many flecks of reflection – you can include one oval of white in each pupil as a stylized representation. Above all, make sure the eyes are as similar and as symmetrical as possible.

3 Next, fill in the hair and the mouth, keeping the hair simple, as shown here. Draw a guide for the hairline, parallel to the top of your circle, but a little farther down the head (no more than a quarter of the height of the circle). Draw small arcs to show the hair is pulled back. Here, a couple of upward-curl bunches have been added. Keep the mouth to one or two lines.

4 The detail on the body, feet and hands is kept to a minimum. Do not labour over the fingers, which can be reduced to a couple of small arcs drawn on to the end of the arms, or even omitted altogether: sometimes a thumb is all you need to suggest a hand. Here the body has been drawn at least two heads tall, but you can go as far as a 1:1 ratio, if you like.

Chibi characters

These cute, simple characters have heads as big or bigger than their bodies. They are often the alter-egos of otherwise normally drawn characters. The chibi styling may be used to show a more childlike side to these characters, which they usually keep hidden.

Two heads in height ◄ ▲
In chibi, childlike proportions are applied not just to the head but to the whole body. If emotion is running high, chibi characters should be drawn as though on the verge of a meltdown.

Three heads in height ▲
Everything about chibi characters is exaggerated, including the hair of the female characters. Emotionally, a chibi character doesn't just feel sad: he or she feels impossibly, gut-wrenchingly sad.

Character themes

Once you are familiar with the basic character types in manga, and understand what they represent and the roles they traditionally play, you can move on from the stereotypes to create characters with unique traits and idiosyncrasies. When you create new characters, it often helps to use ones from existing manga stories as templates, but as their author, you don't have to follow existing rules or create a carbon copy. That's not to suggest you ignore traditional archetypes completely, or your story would hardly be manga, but you could try blending characters from different manga genres to create something fresh and new. Try taking inspiration from other stories you have enjoyed in the past – not just manga,

but favourite films, novels and TV shows. Why are these characters appealing? How can you adapt them for your own use? A character may have a likeable defining trait, which grabs the audience's attention and sympathy immediately, or they may be more complex and mysterious, which can help to keep your audience interested over the long run.

Although the characters on these pages are based on stereotypes, they have been tweaked and altered with more interesting backgrounds and motives, all of which immediately suggest great story ideas. Use them as templates for your first stories, or learn from their example and create your own genre-spanning characters.

Magical Girl with a twist

Magical Girl is a popular protagonist in shojo stories. She is traditionally dressed in a sailor's outfit that is, in fact, a variation on the Japanese schoolgirl uniform. Magical Girls usually have special powers, which they use for good. They obtain their powers from an enchanted object such as a wand, which they keep to undergo a transformation. However, the extent of their powers is normally unclear. The Magical Girl here has been given a twist: she is part-vampire. Is she now the villain of the story? Does she hate who she has become, or has she embraced her vampire side?

Samurai out of time

Samurai characters normally feature in historical stories set in feudal Japan where they encounter black magic and have encounters with strange mythical creatures. But how about a warrior from the future, sent back in time by accident, who becomes a samurai? You could give him a sword of an alloy so strong it can slice through stone. Has your time-travelling samurai found peace in the past and wants to stay, or does he want to find a way back to his own time – at any cost?

Vampiric magic ▶
Though Magic Girl looks sweet on the surface, her uniform is more subdued in colour than usual. Does her wan smile hide sadness – or vicious fangs? Is the wand in her hand a charm to ward off her bloodlust, or a weapon with which to stun her victims?

◀ **Cyborg ronin**
Since this Samurai character is from the future, make him stand out. Here he is a cyborg with superhuman powers: half human, half machine. His armour is a liquid-metal compound that goes rigid when struck, making him unbeatable in single combat.

Trapped in the wrong body

This genius scientist got caught out by his own experiment. Now he's a hamster, and needs to change himself back to human form. He's still a genius, but he's now limited by his size and species. Can he make contact with one of the household children who may be able to help?

Miniature science ▼

The first task of any species-swapped scientist is to replicate his desk at his new scale.

Opposites attract

In a romantic story, your character might be an arrogant man, clever and popular with everyone, but someone who uses people almost without thinking. However, he has a female friend who brings out the best in him, but this side gets lost when there are other people around. As she gets increasingly frustrated by him, what lengths will she go to to get him to change? Is he able to?

Changing for love ▶

What other sides are there to the girl, and does the man, ironically, bring out the worst in her?

Flawed characters

Always limit the strengths and abilities of your protagonists. If they are the best they can ever be from the outset, there is no room for development. A character so skilled and intelligent that he or she never fails, loses a fight, or suffers, will also be dull and one-dimensional. Give your characters flaws because the strongest stories involve overcoming weaknesses, and winning in spite of them.

◀ **Dark alley**
The character shown here has been beaten. He lies on the ground, clutching himself in fear and pain. The three figures in the background stand over him, weapons in hand – are they his cowardly attackers, back to finish the job?

Demon detective

This female detective is from Hell. She catches bad guys, but often in the service of her evil masters. How does she get criminals back to Hades? Was she once human? How does she deflect the suspicion of her colleagues? Notice her hands are gloved. Is she unable to hide her demonic qualities? Do the gloves conceal something grotesque?

Evil for hire ▶

This hard-boiled tale mixes detective procedural with mythical intrigue, giving it an otherworldly element.

Dress to impress

The clothes your characters wear are important to their look, and give your audience a means of recognizing them at all times. When you start formulating your characters, draw them without clothes until you're happy with their shape. Then you can develop their style and dress them up. Clothes move as much and as often as the bodies inside them. Although all fabrics behave differently, they share a tendency to fall away towards gravity and the ground.

Defining status through garments

Clothing not only illustrates fashion choices, age, and wealth or poverty; it can also define the status of a character. A uniform, whether that of the police officer below, a military number, or a nurse's outfit, shows status, rank and authority within society. By contrast, a character dressed in ragged, dirty clothing is likely to live on the streets.

◄ **Sports party**
Equally ready for the tennis court or a beach party, this skimpy ensemble is all about showing off a young and toned physique.

◄ **Baggy style**
The tanktop fits tightly, but everything else is designed for street-corner slouching, or showing off the latest designer names – nonchalantly, of course – in the school halls.

Beat officer ▶
This uniformed police officer and keeper of the peace carries authority around with him just as surely as his baton and portable radio. Nothing about the uniform speaks of 'comfort', only of protection – both for himself and the general public.

Baggy or sporty?

Clothing is a three-dimensional form, and it is through the folds of the clothes that we infer the shading and texture of the fabric. Clothing should still show the shape of the character underneath, however, so don't dress everyone in baggy clothing. Dressing your characters in different ways allows you to suggest depth (or otherwise) in their personalities. A sporty character might wear jogging shorts or a tracksuit, revealing their physique and showing they are in their physical prime. A shy character is likely to wear layers and drab fabrics that push attention away from themselves. Think, too, of the power of a change of clothes: it's not for nothing that many romantic comedies end by unveiling the lead characters in a smart suit or a brand new dress.

Folds

Clothing is relatively taut over body areas that push against fabric. Where there are folds, they form radially, out and away from the bent areas of the body. The five main fold types are described below. To study folds, drape pieces of fabric around different objects to discover where the folds lie.

You'll soon understand how different fabrics form their folds. Essentially, the heavier the material, the more any excess material will fold on itself when hung (although note that skintight clothing won't produce many folds). Always start by sketching in the larger folds, before adding detail.

> **Tip:** When working out how folds hang on a character, picture bracelets around their arms, neck, legs and torso, with the fabric stretched between. As they move, imagine the fabric between each loop bunching and stretching.

Inert/columnesque folds ▲
Each inert fold originates at a point on the waist, and falls to the floor in a conical shape. The columns on the lower right interlock as the dress material gathers on the ground.

Drape folds ▲
These are tall folds that connect across a fabric to form a 'U' shape. The columns lead to the point the fabric is suspended from. Scarves, capes and hoods all show these folds.

Coil folds ▲
These folds occur around cylindrical shapes – typically, the arms, legs and torso, particularly if the material of the clothing is tight. Baggy clothing will not form coil folds.

Interlocking folds ▲
This is where one fold fits inside another. Rolled-up sleeves, large loose-fitting T-shirts, or a scarf wrapped around the neck can all show interlocking folds.

How material hangs

Each of the three items of clothing pictured here show a torso and an arm drawn inside a sleeve. The first top is made from lycra or a similar skintight material, the second is a light cotton sweatshirt, and the third is a thick coat or jacket sleeve. Each fabric shows folds. Watch the way the fabric is being pulled. When clothing is not skintight, material will hang downwards with gravity; but as it is attached to the rest of the fabric worn across the body, it also pulls horizontally away from the arm and upper torso.

Skintight ▲
The fabric stretch is all horizontal, giving defined underarm and elbow creases.

Roomy ▲
Excess fabric bunches towards the forearm but the tight cuff keeps the shape.

Heavy ▲
The thick fabric obscures the shape of the body but is tightly bunched on the arms.

Specific types of clothing

This section looks at some common articles of clothing that you can use to dress up your manga characters. Clothes shape and define their personalities. It's a good idea, at the story planning stage, to make a few notes on what everyone has in their wardrobe. For instance, if your character is school-aged, do they wear a uniform? If not, what is their casual wear?

If they practise a sport, like track and field or a martial art, they should be drawn wearing the appropriate garb – at the very least while they are engaging in it. Bear in mind that most male characters in manga don't wear bright or showy clothes – these are reserved for the females – but that doesn't mean they are not well-presented.

Trousers

Male trousers tend to be loose, whereas female trousers hug the figure. The material on trousers gathers around the waist and top of the thighs (where the leg meets the lower torso), and also around the knees – because if there was no room for manoeuvre there, bending your legs would be an onerous task. Gravity takes care of everything else, which keeps folds to a minimum. If a leg is lifted, for a kick for example, the material folds in a similar way to sleeves. If the trousers are long, folds will rest on the foot.

Skinny trousers ▲
Leaving little to the imagination, skinny trousers are also very light on folds.

Extra-long trousers ▲
The extra material creates a neat fold at the end of each leg but may be bulky.

Baggy trousers ▲
Extra material creates folds around the ankles, where it bunches up and billows out.

Skirts

First, decide on your skirt length and the width (whether you want it loose or tight). When you're ready to draw, start with a simple shape which you can use as a guide; in this case, a blunt cone makes for a stiff miniskirt. To make your skirt less restrictive, add more curve and ripple to the hem. The more you add, the looser it will look – add column folds to show the flow of fabric. Include a slit at the back for a business skirt or at the side (for a more casual appearance). From the front the skirt curves mostly at the side, but at the back it curves outwards with the shape of the body.

Opulent skirt ▲
Just the thing for a cocktail party, this inverted tulip skirt hugs the hips before splaying out into a display of column folds at its base.

From skinny to wide ▲
The business skirt, with slit (left), reveals the shadow of the thighs. The middle skirt hints at column folds, and the final skirt has lots of horizontal movement, suggesting excess fabric.

◀ **Pleated skirt**
For a pleated effect for a school uniform, change the wavy ripples to straight angles, as pleats remove the curve effect, making the skirt appear stiffer.

Practice exercise: Girl's T-shirt

It can often aid your understanding of both the human figure and the fabric you drape upon it if you draw the clothes in isolation, and then apply them. This exercise takes you through the steps.

Materials
• *soft lead pencil*
• *pen and ink*
• *colouring method of your choice*

1 Start by drawing a collar for the neck, using either a 'V' or a circular shape.

2 Add a pair of oval shapes to mark the end of the sleeves, and a small arc at the base of the T-shirt where it will hang to the waist.

3 Draw the connecting lines for the rest of the T-shirt, as well as a few coil folds, as this T-shirt is quite close-fitting.

Tip: Note how the inert T-shirt takes on a number of folds when applied to the figure of the girl. The coil folds on her waist point to her armpits, a shadow in colour delineates her breasts, and drape folds show how the material hangs on the sleeve.

Practice exercise: Cloaks and capes

A cloak or a cape sits on the shoulders, and falls in long straight folds to the floor. These will be mainly column folds, with some drape folds to add texture around the neck. For a military-looking cloak, add thick folds around the shoulders and extend them around to the back.

Materials
• *soft lead pencil*
• *pen and ink*
• *colouring method of your choice*

1 The main body of a cloak is formed from two lines dropped from the shoulders, but the intricate detail starts at the base. Using a wavy line, draw an incomplete crescent for the hem, as above.

2 Now draw a tapered vertical line leading upwards from a point on every curve. At this stage your cloak will look strangely translucent.

Tip: It's a good idea to collect reference from fashion catalogues and magazines, and to model your outfits accordingly. If your story is set in a fantasy or futuristic setting, you can be more daring and inventive, but make sure you keep some elements which are easy to relate to.

3 Now erase the lines and curves hidden by the folds of the cloak, or the human figure within it. The cloak is clasped on either side of the neck, while the hood is formed from a rough oval, with its peak in the centre of the forehead. If in doubt about the hood's shape, try sketching yourself in a hooded top.

Clothing gallery

If there's one visual arena in which manga is unreservedly triumphant, it's in bringing high fashion to its heroes and heroines. Whether fighting off demons in between advanced algebra classes or piloting enormous mecha into battle against a faceless alien horde, manga characters are always at the cutting edge of contemporary clothing – a fact lovingly acknowledged by the legions of 'Cosplayers' who dress up at conventions as their favourite manga icons.

The infinite wardrobe

When the detail on your manga character's faces is limited by the simplicity of the form, the complexity and nuance you can add through their clothing takes on a greater dimension. Think of the ways clothing is used in society. A T-shirt with a slogan can offer insight into a character's politics – as does their choice of a T-shirt over a suit and tie. Think as well of clothes that a character is forced to wear: uniforms, whether for school or work. How do they wear these cookie-cutter costumes? With pride? In a slovenly fashion? Have they made rule-breaking customizations to the length of the skirt or the knot in the tie? This attitude is as important as the clothes themselves.

Café maid ▼
This brightly coloured maid's costume suggests a bizarre, almost doll's house-like drinking establishment.

Everyday casual ◀
The standard uniform of relaxed people everywhere.

Gothic teenage girl ▲
The striped stockings and puffed shorts and sleeves draw inspiration from a mishmash of classical styles. The purple makes this perfect for a witch or vampire-in-training.

Head waiter ▶
The opulent, burgundy apron and cravat suggest the waiter is serving at an exceptionally posh restaurant. Even without a character inhabiting these clothes, what are they saying? Do you get the sense of a snooty establishment, or of good service?

◄ **Rock star or pirate?**
With the pointed collars of a rock star, this character will charm hearts – or wallets – in a lifetime of swashbuckling adventure.

Milkmaid outfit ▲
The pepper-pot shape suggests comic relief – or a school board totally without humour.

Future biker ◄
Tight-fitting, heavy-duty leathers allow for spectacular street races.

Flowerprint dress ▲
The larger cut, flowers and subdued colours of this dress suggest this is the costume of the lead girl's less ostentatious friend.

Reserved rock chick ▶
Though a stiff breeze may blow this kooky character over by day, at night she stalks the karaoke bars, putting together the ultimate band from fellow karaoke addicts.

◄ **Skater chic**
The wearer of these clothes would be equally at home on a skateboard or BMX, or at least they would like you to think so. The loose-fitting clothes would also suit a street-ninja in training, or a contemporary boy hurled through to another dimension.

Character accessories

Once you have decided on your characters' clothing, you can also choose some accessories as further embellishment. The objects your characters keep on and about their person will add depth to their individual personalities. You will want to ensure that your audience can easily identify your lead characters, which is sometimes difficult in mainly black and white narratives without these smaller details. Accessorizing your characters will help make your creations unique, so that readers will know them from their appearance alone. Everyday technological gadgets that can offer a window into new storytelling possibilities, or just add an extra veneer of cool to your tech-savvy protagonists.

Ribbons, headbands and glasses

Female manga characters often wear ribbons in their hair, and the addition of a ribbon is often a clue to a character's age. Large ribbons tied around bunches, for example, will suggest a younger character, as will a single large bow around a ponytail. If you show a girl's hair tied in bunches, you also have the option to include long strands of excess ribbon dangling down with the hair. A sophisticated hairband tends to age up a character. The girl shown last could be a college activist, or on a 'gap year' adventure. Glasses are often used to say something about a character.

Pink bow ▲
A large bow on a pony tail makes a character look cute, innocent and young.

Hairband ▲
With hair out of her eyes, this older character is ready for business.

Glasses ▲
These add interest to the face and can be used as a disguise, to suggest scholarly tendencies – or just to improve bad eyesight.

Rings, bracelets, symbols and belts

From the grinning skulls of secret college organizations to the cheap plastic of a trinket given as a party favour, you can tell a lot about your characters from what jewellery they wear; not least of which, whether they are married or not – or whether they bear a signet or decoder ring that marks them out as a king or a spy.

Emblems can have meanings that are significant in a story. Belts can carry potions or messages, images of loved ones or carefully scribed spells. Make each accessory unique with meaningful symbols, patterns, studs or precious stones.

Finger jewellery ▲
Rings can reflect characters' histories. Where did they get them? Were they a gift? Do they have more than sentimental value?

Symbols ▲
What family treasures and secrets are locked up in these emblems?

Belt with pouches ▲
Handed down from warrior to warrior, a belt can contain battlefield herbs and medications.

Mobile phone

Many shonen stories feature characters who have a penchant for gadgets and gizmos, so it helps to keep abreast of the latest developments in technology, drawing inspiration from the hottest designs to build your own creations. You may want to push the possibilities of modern technology, incorporating fantastic features. You may have a mobile phone yourself, so finding reference to practise from shouldn't be a problem. Furthermore, visiting the websites of major brands will allow you to view their available phones, often accompanied by interactive 3-D demonstrations. Tilt the reality of your story by adding more features to your invented models. Phones today can make video calls, take photos, play music and track position by GPS. Police or military characters could use mobiles for more than just calls, tracking down criminals with their cameras. Other useful features include infrared capability, or limited hologram generation. Programs could be voice-operated, or the mobile could have artificial intelligence.

Simple handset ▲
Start with a rectangular cuboid. Keep the scale of the device around the same size as your character's hand.

Media handset ▲
The standard handset is streamlined, given a bigger screen and updated with more advanced capabilities.

Laptop and headset

In many ways, aside from the scale, drawing a laptop is much the same as drawing a mobile phone, in that it involves a screen and buttons that can be drawn with a simple grid method. Make sure the screen is of a size with the bottom half, so that they lock together when the 'clamshell' is closed.

Don't forget some simple cylinders to show how the monitor is hinged on to the keyboard. Practise drawing the laptop open and closed. If it is a piece of equipment used regularly by a character, you should consider personalizing it. Think about using a shape unique to that character, or give it a logo, sticker or custom stencil that denotes ownership. The laptop can also be customized with peripherals. With the headset you could make the computer obey voice commands. This could make for some interesting dialogue if you show a super-smart human character verbally interacting with an advanced computer.

Standard laptop ▲
A common modern laptop – an excellent jumping-off point for your own creation.

Hands-free headset ▲
Perfect for delivering voice commands or having a conversation while on the run, or delivering a commentary during an action-based adventure.

◄ **Ultra-light kit**
This boy genius has built from scratch an ultra-light laptop with the processing power of multiple supercomputers. The headset is part of communicating voice commands.

Weapons

Fighting weapons are intrinsic to manga, and play an important role in identifying the principal characters. Regardless of genre, most main characters possess a method of fighting that makes them stand out. They may fight with a sword, a gun, a magical power, or by practising a martial art (sometimes in combination with a weapon, i.e. 'gun fu', or by using a characteristic and empowering piece of armour, clothing or jewellery).

Practice exercise: Drawing a gun

Guns come in a range of sizes and styles, and can be constructed with geometric shapes. Put some thought into why your character uses a gun: what it fires (bullets or some sort of beam?); whether they are skilful or a liability with a gun in their hand. You can also personalize the weapon by giving it an unusual barrel, or markings on the grip.

Materials
- cartridge paper
- blue pencil 10
- pen and ink
- colour of your choice

1 Sketch guides, keeping to basic rectangular shapes: a standard sidearm is formed of three tilted rectangles, as shown.

2 Draw in the first stage of detail. Pay attention to the way the parts interlock, and the curved elements that interrupt the angular silhouette.

3 Add further details, such as the ridging on the stock. Draw the items as they are, not how you might expect them to be.

4 When you are happy with your pencilled lines, ink your illustration.

5 Finish off the gun by colouring it using the method of your choice. Add contrasts between the burnished metal parts and the textured handgrip.

Practice exercise: Sword basics

In the Arthurian legend of the Round Table, the sword Excalibur was as much a symbol that bound the knights together for the good of the country, as it was the ultimate weapon. In Japanese legends, the sword is also laden with symbology: promises are sworn upon the sword – and if vengeance is sworn, then it is always delivered with honour.

Materials
- cartridge paper
- red pencil
- pen and ink
- colour of your choice

1 Start with a gentle curve, forming the base line of your sword. Arc it up gently at the right, for the hilt, and more sharply towards the tip of the blade, at the left. The red pencil line reminds you of the proportions of the sword length.

2 For this sword, keep the width of the blade the same as the width of the hilt. Draw a line down the centre of the blade to show the two edges of the sword, and add a handguard just over two-thirds down. Add a pattern on the hilt, using repeated thin ellipses.

3 Ink your pencil lines when you are ready. As with the gun, you may wish to use a technical pen for the blade, although an organic line would suit the woven fibres on the hilt. Colour the sword using the method of your choice, suggesting the sharpness of the metal with strong white highlights. Ensure that one edge of the sword is darker than the other, to show that they are angled differently.

Other types of gun

There are other types of gun, of course. You could choose a magnum, a revolver, a pump-action shotgun, a machine gun or a sniper's rifle. Practise drawing them at many different angles.

Shotgun

Rifle

Revolver

Mêlée weapon effects

Close combat weapons are called mêlée weapons. They are a great accessory for any warrior character, but their dynamism can be vastly increased with a number of simple effects – both motion-based and magical. See how you can transform a simple clash of swords into an epic battle worthy of titans with the addition of just a few speed lines.

Axe

Straight-edge axe

Dagger

Spear

Bow

Sword

Motion lines ▶
Fine lines of motion increase the drama of a sword swing, indicating the trajectory of the weapon and the speed at which it is being swung. The longer the lines and the closer they are packed together, the more extreme the motion. Draw your lines tracing back from the blade of the sword to the beginning of its arc. Speedlines will often overlap with the background art, although you may find a stark white panel, isolating the character and the sword swing, could prove more effective.

Magical glow ▲
Eldritch energy wraps around this ethereal blade, immediately telling us that the weapon is out of the ordinary and possessed of magical powers. As well as striking fear into the hearts of its foes, the sword also suggests story possibilities – where did it come from, what powers does it possess, and who held it before the current wielder?

Tip: Sometimes the use of motion lines isn't appropriate, particularly if the panel already features speedlines in the background. The two will just mix into one another and muddy the action. Instead, use a white absence of lines to show the trajectory of motion, either erasing the background speedlines in the appropriate arc, or drawing two lines surrounding a single broad streak. This will look much clearer within an already busy shot.

Impact effects ▶
This image combines the dynamism of motion lines with an explosive illustration of the point of impact. The still panel illustrates a full, fluid movement. As the eye moves down the panel, we see the arc of the sword, its impact against the haft of the spear, and the impact throwing the spearman backwards. Fiery colours draw the eye to the most important action.

Putting it together

Now that you've learned how to build human and non-human characters from the inside out, and populated dozens of wardrobes and armouries with clothes and devastating new weapons, it's time to combine these strands into a pair of fully realized characters. The following two practice exercises guide you through the process of character creation for both a male and female protagonist, from concept to colour. The two characters are from very different genres – the male from a downbeat, futuristic action thriller and the female from a high-fantasy, magical shojo adventure. The steps taken in their creation are very similar. Why not create a complementary character for each setting?

Practice exercise: Post-apocalyptic bounty hunter

This character wanders the post-apocalyptic wasteland of America after a ruthless bio-weapon strike killed 85 per cent of the population with a gene-bomb virus. In the ruins of society, he helps maintain the fragile grip of law, rounding up escaped prisoners and delivering them to the last vestiges of government. He is growing increasingly ambivalent about his job, and is beginning to think he is just propping up a corrupt administration that could be replaced by something better.

1 Start the drawing off with a loose sketch of the proportions. Keep the character lanky and tall, and the stance powerful even when standing still. Position the hands to hold a weapon.

Materials
- *cartridge paper*
- *blue pencil 10*
- *pen and ink*
- *colours of your choice*

2 Begin to rough in some of the details – add loose-fitting desertwear clothing and a tattered cloak. Show the direction of the desert winds by blowing the long hair and cloak out backwards. Add plenty of pouches for ammunition and supplies across the chest, and tightly bind the feet and legs in bandages.

3 Firm up your favourite lines, and sharpen your detail. Add focus to the image with areas of shadow around the eyes and underneath the throat. Change the silhouette of the cloak, adding tears, ripped areas and new folds. Customize the gunstock and concentrate effort on the character's gauntlets and belts.

Tip: Limited colour schemes, such as the warm browns and reds on the bounty hunter are often the most effective, as they generate a coherent mood around a character. It is also easier to create contrasting background effects against a character in a narrow range of hues.

4 When you have inked your drawing, colour it, using muted, earthy tones, with cool spots of blue and green to break up and define the character's shape. Draw focus to the head with a softened blood red for the hair.

Practice exercise: Precipitation Faerie

This elfin character is one of the hundreds of elemental faeries tasked with seeing that the natural world runs as it is supposed to. The Precipitation Faerie is part of a task force charged with making sure the rain cycle continues. Along with her sisters in the Evaporation and Condensation departments, she travels around the globe, puncturing stubborn clouds, encouraging recalcitrant droplets and doing her best to see that the 'rain in Spain falls mainly on the plain' (among other plateau platitudes). She takes her job very seriously, but enjoys taking time off to soak up the sun, up above the clouds.

Materials
• cartridge paper
• pen and ink
• colours of your choice

2 Sketch in some clothing. Here we've gone for a Gothic yet girlish-style ruffled dress, puffy sleeves and a hat, not to mention some killer platform heels, a lace-up corset and fringed gloves. The faerie's magical umbrella begins to take shape as a bowl – a similar shape to her hairstyle.

1 Start with a simple anatomical sketch, as before. We've gone for very skinny limbs and a classic pin-up/Busby Berkeley dancer pose, with a large head that will be mostly hair in the final piece. Keep the limbs long and the figure lithe.

3 Add in the final pencilled details, adding tone and texture to the sleeves and the ruffles of the dress. Create some softly veined wings, and expand the umbrella's bowl shape with ridged 'wavelets'. Keep the faerie's face very simple – taut lips, a vertical line for the nose, and wide eyes closely framed by the detail of her hair.

4 The final colour version adds a swirl of blue rain-magic emanating from the tip of the umbrella, along with a number of interesting 'colour holds' (when black lines are exchanged for colour) on the outlines of the translucent wings and on the ruffles of the black dress in particular. The areas of exposed skin contrast sharply with the narrow range of blues and blacks of the clothing, while the magical elements of the wings and the swirl of rain share the same bright turquoise.

Kodomo animal characters

Another popular manga genre is that of anthropomorphic animal stories. These feature animals with human qualities: they walk upright, talk, wear clothes and behave like people. Anthropomorphic stories are successful on a number of counts: the simpler, animal-based drawings are 'attractive' to a large number of readers; they allow for commentary on the human condition by showing common foibles in a new light; and they allow for humorous juxtapositions in more adult stories by showing 'childhood favourites' in mature or compromising situations. Kodomo characters can also be subjected to extremes of violence without gore or consequences, an orgy of cartoonish slapstick. Don't feel that kodomo stories need to be throwaway or totally lightweight, however: think about the most enduring cartoon characters and most memorable stories – how many feature humans, and how many anthropomorphs?

Kodomo characters visually share a lot with super-deform characters – they are based on exaggerated and compacted human anatomy, with simple, engaging facial features incorporating streamlined elements of their animal forms. For instance, the tiger and the rabbit below have similar facial structures, eyes and ears, despite being very different in real life. When in doubt, strip out detail rather than adding it in. We will create some of the inhabitants of a shady downtown bar, all of which just happen to be cute animals with drinking problems and a world of gripes.

Tiger footballer ▲
Not the smartest toy in the box, this tiger looks half asleep. His football boots and strip indicate to us that his strength may lie on the pitch.

Bunny engineer ▲
The dungarees indicate this jolly rabbit is a clock-repairer and electronics whiz. She could even be tied up in trading secrets in acts of industrial espionage.

Practice exercise: Bad-tempered bat

This character is oblivious to the world around him. His brow is furrowed and his eyes squinting. His exaggerated form is very simple: vicious jags for wings, two enormous ears jutting out of a potato-shaped head, and spindly limbs folded across a similarly dumpy body. A range of unexpected accoutrements add extra flavour: head tattoos and facial hair, multiple extreme piercings, comedy flip-flops and the exceptional dress sense of a Wall Street banker on a summer holiday.

Materials
• *soft lead pencil*
• *pen and ink*
• *colouring method of your choice*

1 Roughly sketch in all the details of the bat, using simple, expressive shapes. Focus on the overall shapes rather than specificities at this stage.

2 Make your details more specific, keeping the eyes big and the rest of the facial features small. Work up your sketch into a finished inked piece.

3 Colour your bat with flat tones, emphasizing his more bizarre characteristics in bright colours.

Practice exercise: Drunken penguin

Here's another patron to adorn your bar: a drunken penguin, drowning the sorrows of his failing business in one,

Materials
- *soft lead pencil*
- *pen and ink*
- *colouring method of your choice*

two or three bottles of mid-price wine. His glasses, hat and coat all suggest a middle-aged businessman of some social standing, so perhaps this is the first time he's stumbled into a shadowy bar. Alternatively, perhaps he's a frequent feature at the bar: a professional drunk who turns up in

a slightly tatty jacket every Friday night. Nobody knows where he comes from, but he has an anthology of rambling, slurred stories to entertain the rest of the bar with.

1 Sketch in the basic features. The penguin starts as an obese skittle. The 'jacket' feathers of a real penguin are turned into an actual suit jacket.

2 Ink the lines, adding characterful details like the pocket handkerchief, checked hatband and empty bottle brandished like a truncheon.

3 Add visual interest at the colour stage by using bright blue and yellow instead of the real penguin's monochrome scheme.

Developing the characters

Your anthropomorphic world may need no explanation: the characters might just be talking animals instead of people. You may want to incorporate your world into our own, however: perhaps it's a secret bar for soft toys, who visit it for a beverage and a whine when their children owners are asleep. Perhaps it's the only place where they can escape from toddler drool or sadistic next-door neighbours and be themselves – and if that means eight or twelve pints before the sun comes up, then so be it ...

Raising the bar ▶
The shady basement bar contrasts amusingly with the bright forms and pleasing shapes of the anthropomorphic creatures. Despite the childish appearance, these are adult themes.

Girl protagonist project

This is how to create a protagonist who could front either a shonen or shojo story. We'll also show how to develop a character concept beyond your initial sketches and into an actual storyline. Shonen and shojo have basic similarities: in each, the protagonist is trying to reach a goal, bettering themselves along the way. Shonen stories do this through action-oriented means, while shojo utilizes more contemplative, psychological narratives about relationships. For our example, we've chosen a character who can shine in either genre: a musician. As a female lead, she can be involved with either genre – perhaps as the vocalist and guitarist for an otherwise all-male band.

Your choice of genre will determine how you build the surrounding characters and storyline. A shojo story may feature a band with more introspective, acoustic music, with the thrust of the story being the interpersonal relationships between band members and the way in which the songwriter's life informs her lyrics. A shonen story, by contrast, could focus on a punkier, more aggressive band battling to get signed by a record company, showcasing the rivalry between your characters and other bands that also want the prize. This rivalry could spill over into action-packed set pieces or physical confrontations.

Materials
- *soft lead pencil*
- *pen and ink*
- *colouring method of your choice*

Ready to rock ▶

Clothing, hair, tattoos and accessories combine to create a very strong sense of character, even without reading a single line of her dialogue.

1 Once you've settled on your character type and done a little research, begin your figure with a stick frame pose. The pose here incorporates the guitar, directing attention towards it and adding a centre to the pose. She's wielding an electric guitar.

2 Flesh out the character's outline and start adding detail to the guitar – place the hands and fingers at this stage. Block in all of the proportions, paying attention to the joints and the way the body curves along the action line to accommodate the instrument.

3 Focus on the character's facial characteristics and rough anatomy next, defining the details of the head. Keep the hair tomboyish and relatively short. Make her attractive and independent: confident in her abilities and strong despite her physical slightness.

4 Add in clothing, using the anatomy as a guide to where her T-shirt and trousers will fold. Think not only of the clothes she will be wearing, but how she will be wearing them – are they loose or tightly fitted? Are they customized? Are they worn sloppily or smartly?

Developing the character

Later, you could create a unique twist on your character as your story develops, testing them with tragedy or misfortune. One idea could give your protagonist the means to play riffs no other band has ever achieved – a bionic arm. Your guitarist could lose their flesh-and-blood arm in a terrible accident, leaving them fearful they would never play again. A shojo story would show the singer's slow rehabilitation, with the tears and triumphs along the way as they learn to play again. The arm could be the result of a top-secret bionic experiment, which gives them the ability to play better and faster – but getting there won't be easy; you'll want to keep your audience on your side.

Finally, think about the rest of the band. How many members? What instruments would they play? Think about how they react to the protagonist, either with or without the bionic arm. Their history: have they ever broken up before? Is every rehearsal a drama? If your story is mainly about the band, the other members will be your secondary characters, driving the interpersonal relationships and dramas in between gigs.

5 Here, we've gone for long and baggy trousers, lined with multiple pockets, and covered in zips and belts. Her T-shirt has her favourite album cover screen-printed on to it – you could compose it in a separate image using Photoshop, drawing an album cover of your own at a larger size and then reducing and deforming it to fit. Further accessories include leather wristbands, a choker, and a lightning-bolt necklace on a long chain.

6 When you've completed your inks, colour the image, paying close attention to the textures of the fabrics, the tones of her face, and the various shines and glinting effects on the guitar. Remember that her aim is to shock and attract attention, so don't shy away from bright, clashing colours like pinks and greens. A tattoo on her right arm completes the look.

Tip: Investigate magazines and websites of your character's chosen subculture in order to research ideas for their clothing and accessories. In this instance, music magazines, websites and videos all informed the look of the rocker, but the same would apply if your character was an army colonel, a sports idol, or an astronaut. Don't just slavishly copy clothing; add your own unique twists to basic fashion styles in order to make your protagonists stand out.

Changing the look ▲
Depending on your story, the addition of a bionic limb could be creepy – or a triumph of the human spirit.

Cyborg close-up ▲
The new limb follows the same skeletal structure as an actual arm, only without musculature or skin on top.

Fantasy pirate project

Piracy has made a return to a variety of comics, including manga, helped by the popularity of films like *Pirates of the Caribbean* and the pirate-rich computer games in the *Monkey Island* series. The manga *One Piece*, for instance, features a rag-tag group of freebooters seeking the treasure of the King of the Pirates. In this character project you'll create your own tyrant of the high seas.

This character needs to be feared and mysterious, surrounded at all times by grand legend and whispered hearsay.

pirates live, thrive and die by their dark and devious reputations, relying on tales recounted over grog to keep lesser sailors quaking in their hammocks, dreaming of sighting their tattered masts and skull-and-crossbones flag on the horizon. While most pirates are ruthless in hand-to-hand combat, instilling fear in others is their greatest weapon.

Materials
- *soft pencil*
- *pen and ink*
- *colouring method of your choice*

Cut-throat villain ▶
An imposing force of nature, this pirate captain – veteran of 35 sea battles and sinker of 13 merchant vessels – is not to be messed with. His finery, though ripped and repaired, is nonetheless the most valuable on his vessel. He wears his scars and bandages with fearsome pride.

1 Begin as usual with a sketched frame for the character, outlining the basic shape of the limbs and the stance. Here, the pirate is brandishing a large cutlass ahead of him. As a villain of some stature, he needs to be drawn at least eight to nine heads high.

2 Start to flesh out the character by roughing in the true anatomy and drawing in the clothing. Take the opportunity to add an unconventional twist to 'traditional' pirate clothing from the 17th and 18th centuries. Pay attention to the various folds around the sleeves, cuffs, collar and knees, and note how the various sashes influence the folds around them. The oversized boot-tops, collar, cuffs and hat all create an imposing, almost inhuman silhouette. The asymmetry of the ripped trouser leg, bicep sash and facial bandages increase the captain's uniqueness and make him look less like the result of a pirate assembly line.

3 As you tighten up your rough lines and begin adding in detail, focus on the face. Shadowed beneath the hat, with intriguing bandages hinting at disfigurement, eyes are immediately drawn to the face. Keep the expression a simple snarl, letting the bandages do the talking.

4 Continue to work up the details of your character, filling in the silhouette. Clothing is broken up with folds, and accentuated with straps, bandages, belts and ties. This character is already quite busy, art-wise, so you don't need to accessorize him too much. Being a famous pirate, however, he will arm himself well. As well as the cutlass, which is customized and given expensive-looking detailing at this stage, we've added a flintlock pistol in his right hand. Use an encyclopaedia, history book or Internet search to find reference for historical weaponry you can use as inspiration. When in doubt, exaggerate the size of any swords, and add complex gilting and ornamentation worthy of a pirate captain's status. Here, as if having both hands full weren't enough, there are also spare daggers tucked into his belt.

5 When you're satisfied with your pencils, ink them and move on to colour. As with the rock star on the previous page, the pirate is all about shock, awe and a monstrous first impression, so keep the colours bright, save for the deadly colours on the hat and boots. The red and purple coat suggests villainous royalty.

Developing the character

With your first colour draft of the character complete, you can now begin to flesh out his history and surroundings. Where did he come from? How did he rise up the pirate ranks, and which other pirates did he gut in order to reach the top? Try placing your character in context, drawing him with a background of a huge skull-and-crossbones flag, or, if you're feeling more confident, at the prow of his own jet-black ship, or standing in his cabin, inspecting his amassed trunk of loot.

Everything about your illustration suggests new story possibilities. Why is his face bandaged? Are they recent wounds, received in a sword-fought brawl for the captaincy? Or have the scars long since faded, the bandages kept on as a reminder of one moment of weakness? Perhaps he was hideously scarred by fire as a child; a concept that could tie into his reasons for becoming a terror of the high seas, taking as much as he can from a world that stripped him of any possibility of a normal life. It could also be a form of disguise. Anyone who meets the pirate captain will remember his piercing eyes and

bandages, but little else. When the captain reaches port, he untwines the bandages and can walk among the harbour folk without drawing attention to himself. He could even be an undercover agent of the Crown!

Once your character's background is established, try to flesh out the world in which he lives – who are his crew, and how did he recruit them? What challenges exist for the dark king of the sea? This could be everything from a ship of rival pirates, to mythological beasts like the kraken (an enormous sea monster), on to a naval task force that has been tasked with bringing the pirate to trial.

Early days ▶
Just one of hundreds of possibilities – here we see the pirate on his first tour of duty, before he rose up the ranks and received his scars.

Building the backgrounds

Once we have our principal players, we need to locate them in the world of the narrative. But what kind of world do you want to create? Is your setting the past, the present day, or the future? Will you set your tale in a land of fantasy, or in the world around you? Here, we'll look at the creation of manga worlds, from basic drawing tips to imaginative flights of fancy.

Background and perspective

Characters cannot exist without backgrounds and settings to ground them, provide visual interest and colour, and show where characters exist in relation to one another. Backgrounds are often fiddly and time-consuming to draw, so many manga artists tend to minimize them or leave them out altogether when they are just starting out. But backgrounds are essential to gripping manga stories: just try to picture an epic like *Akira* without its sprawling cityscapes. Don't be discouraged, however, by the insane amount of detail in such books – a simpler approach will often work just as well. Think of the difference between a shot of a well-illustrated character leaping through the air against an empty white panel – and the same character image placed against the backdrop of an enormous ravine. Judicious use of backdrops and scenery amps up the drama of your stories and makes panel-to-panel storytelling clearer. Illustrating backgrounds involves learning about the basics of settings and perspective, which is where this spread comes in.

The horizon line

Where the ground seems to meet the sky is known as the horizon line. It is always at eye level from our personal point of view. This fact is also incredibly useful when drawing a number of different characters in a panel. No matter how close or how far away the characters are, draw them so their eyes are all bisected by the horizon line and they will always be in the correct perspective in relation to one another. Make use of the horizon as an excellent 'default' perspective for your stories.

◀ **One-point perspective**
The tracks and electricity poles diminish towards a single 'vanishing point' on the horizon – the point at which no further details can be seen. This is perspective's simplest form. To ensure your dimensions are correct, sketch in straight guide lines radiating out from the vanishing point.

Point of view

Often abbreviated as 'POV', this marks the point at which your 'camera' is placed to view the events you are drawing. Depending on how close or far away from your action you place this point, the objects and people under scrutiny may appear smaller or larger.

Your point of view can also be placed above or below the horizon line, changing the angles of view and potentially introducing additional vanishing points to complicate – and add drama – to your perspective. Perspective is the term used to describe how points drawn from distant shapes fall on the 'picture plane' (imagining your flat pages as 'windows' in a three-dimensional space) from your chosen point of view. The examples below show how different POVs change how objects appear.

Lines converge equally on the picture plane

Distortion introduced as taller points now produce longer lines

Angled POV increases distortion

◀ **POV examples**:
Note how the buildings appear to stretch and recede upwards as the POV gets closer to them. From a distance, their shape can be viewed with little distortion: each point converges on the eye equally. With the POV nearer, some points are closer to the POV than others: the closer points appear larger.

Perspective

Depth perception in art is an illusion; since you are using a two-dimensional medium to suggest three dimensions. You will notice that, in the examples shown here, all of the objects appear to get smaller and smaller as they recede farther back into the picture plane, until they 'disappear' at the vanishing point. While many artists had previously understood that objects appear larger the closer to the POV they stand, and smaller when farther away. It wasn't until the Renaissance that the concept of the vanishing point and the

mathematical ability to replicate the perspectives of reality on a flat surface became widely used. It was the Florentine architect Brunelleschi who first observed the vanishing point, as well as the 16th-century painter Albrecht Dürer, also a pioneer on human proportion, who invented the notion of the 'picture plane'. Dürer achieved this by drawing objects he observed through, and on to, a piece of glass. Perspective affects more than perception of size, it also causes objects to appear closer together the farther

away they get – consider the difference between looking at a city on the horizon, when all you can see is a clump of buildings, and flying over that same city, when the morass of shapes separates out into clearly delineated buildings. In our everyday lives the picture plane is what we observe through our eyes. When drawing, the plane falls on the medium where the drawing is made. In the next section we'll take a look at more complex perspectives, using multiple vanishing points, in more detail.

> **Tip:** Perspective isn't just about showing off your technical ability and altering the way you show and establish buildings and characters. Altering your perspectives works best as a dramatic device to add impact to a beat of your story. Think how much more menacing a school bully appears when framed from a worm's eye view, or how terrifying the drop from a cliff if you can see all the way down to the raging sea and the rocks below. Think how everyday actions can be shown in a new and intriguing light.

Worm's-eye view (three-point perspective) ▲
A worm's-eye view keeps the focus tightly on the building at the centre of your panel. It's great for establishing scale, even menace, as an edifice towers over the reader's point of view.

Bird's-eye view (three-point perspective) ▲
This overhead perspective is perfect for vertiginous, scene-setting panels, looking down on a location (in this instance, a townhouse) from a very high point. This perspective allows you to show a lot of detail in the area surrounding the panel's focus – meaning additional drawing time for the artist, but time well spent in establishing a neighbourhood as an important location.

Cropping and framing (single-point perspective) ▲
Here, the vanishing point is outside of the right-hand boundary of the panel. This is a more realistic framing of a scene, as we don't always see the terminus of a perspective line in real life. When drawing a panel such as this, you may wish to experiment by extending your guide lines beyond the panel, or using a fixed point off the page entirely to anchor your construction marks. See if this makes a difference.

Vanishing acts

When drawing anything in perspective you need to know about the three different vanishing point constructs that will allow you to convey a sense of depth and realism from an infinite variety of angles. Remember that within a lot of the panels of your story you will be trying to maintain a decent perspective so that an essentially two-dimensional medium can be forced to feel three-dimensional. For the examples below, you will need a ruler, as drawing them freehand will probably make them uneven. If you don't want to judge the angles by eye also use a protractor when drawing the lines from each vanishing point.

Practice exercise: Single vanishing point

In a single-point perspective, the point of view and vanishing point form the two extremes of the same straight line.

1 Start by drawing a horizon line, and then add a vanishing point in the centre of the line. This is where all the lines, aside from the vertical, will appear to be pointing. All the lines converging to this point can be above or below the horizon line.

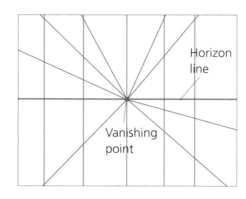

Materials
- *HB pencil*
- *ruler and protractor*
- *pen and ink*
- *colouring method of your choice*

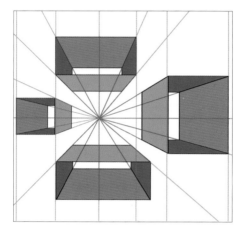

2 Use your horizon line and vanishing point to draw a cube that appears to recede into the distance. Draw straight lines fanning out from the vanishing point to help you get the outline for the cube. The lines that form the front and back of the cube are parallel or at right angles to the horizon. If a cube is below the horizon line we are looking down on it (as below the horizon line, straight ahead, represents below our eye level). If you draw the lines above the horizon line, it is above our eye line, and therefore we look up to the cube.

Practice exercise: Two-point perspective

In a two-point perspective the use of two vanishing points means that only the vertical lines used will be parallel to each other. Essentially this is like standing at the vanishing point of a single-point perspective and looking back. The two-point perspective allows you to make objects appear at an angle rather than face on (as seen in the previous example). If you draw the two-point perspective above the horizon line you will once again be looking up at the object. Two-point perspectives are also useful for drawing interiors as well as exteriors.

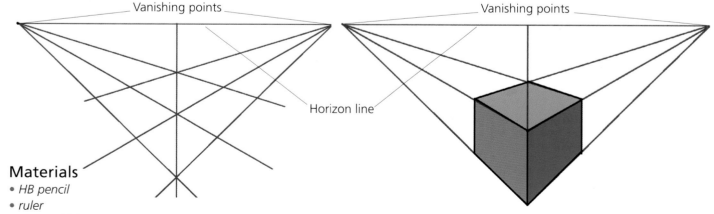

Materials
- *HB pencil*
- *ruler*
- *pen and ink*
- *colouring method of your choice*

1 Start with the horizon line again, but mark your vanishing points at either end of the line.

2 Draw lines fanning out from the points, below the horizon line, towards you. This will create a series of new guide lines for the shape you'll create in the centre. You're drawing below the horizon line, so you will be looking down on the shape. Invert the guide lines to look up at a shape.

Practice exercise: Three vanishing points

This technique is particularly useful if you want to emphasize the height or depth of something. Start by creating two points, the same as the previous example, but place an additional third point either above or below the horizon line. For this version keep it below the exact centre of the horizon line.

Materials
- *HB pencil*
- *ruler*
- *pen and ink*
- *colouring method of your choice*

> **Tip:** Remember that the use of 'mathematical' perspective in manga is a guide, not an unbreakable rule. Breaking the boundaries can produce more artistic, exaggerated or dramatic results.

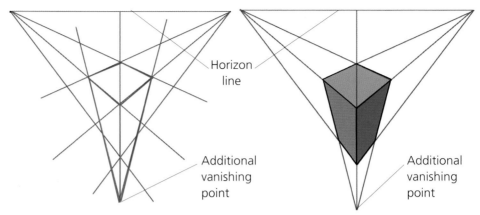

Horizon line

Additional vanishing point

Additional vanishing point

1 Once you've crafted a square in two-point perspective, draw diagonal lines from the left and right corners to the third vanishing point below, creating the corner that will face you directly. This creates an inverted pyramid, or, actually, a cuboid box that diminishes to the vanishing point.

2 Placing the third vanishing point above the horizon line will create a pyramid in the opposite direction, looking up towards the peak from its base. Although the example here shows a finished cuboid shape, the perspective guide lines will help you draw any shape – from any angle.

Looking up and down

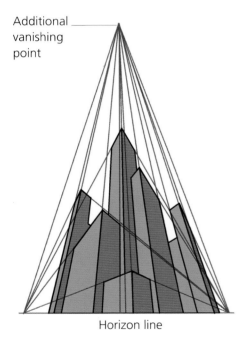

Additional vanishing point

Horizon line

The use of an extreme three-point perspective is essential to creating vertiginous cityscapes for your characters to run, swing or drive through. You can quickly move on to more intricate designs by placing the horizon line at the base of the page, with the third vanishing point as high up the page as possible. Start with your two horizon points at the bottom of the page. Draw two main lines from them to the central third vanishing point. Draw a few more faint lines from along the horizon line to the third point, and cross those lines with lines fanning out from the two horizon vanishing points. By drawing over these sketchy lines, you will be able to form your perspective guides into solid geometric shapes, and from there, into fully realized buildings.

Horizon line

Additional vanishing point

Worm's-eye view ▲

Create a few 3-D shapes that seem to jut out of the main structure, bearing in mind that to make them stand out they'll need their own corners, using a line from the left-hand horizon point, a line from the right horizon point, and a line from the top horizon point to intersect the two shapes going up the page; use the example above to help you. Try to create a few of your own as well, as it will help you understand the process. Using photo reference – perhaps of a New York street – see if you can increase the level of complexity on your basic shapes, adding windows, ledges, gargoyles and the like, to test and extend your understanding.

Bird's-eye view ▲

This process can be reversed, with the horizon at the top of the page, to look down on a cityscape as from some mountaintop eyrie. It's a simple case of creating your geometric structures heading downwards, instead of up.

Placing characters

You have already created a single vanishing point and a horizon line. Now we will look at this type of perspective in detail, where to use multiple-point perspective, and how to plan and place characters when you draw the background first. When you're constructing a scene with both background and characters, you must ensure that the perspectives match. This is important with a street scene, for example, with multiple people walking around, as the sizes of the characters must correspond to where they are standing, and with the perspective used. Remember the eyes of your characters will pass through the horizon line (unless they have a significant height difference and are standing next to one another; see pages 28–31). If you don't pay attention to these details, your characters may end up bending the laws of physics. This is important with body parts (feet, for example) that extend outside a panel's boundary.

Practice exercise: Multiple vanishing points

This exercise strips away the backgrounds to show how to draw characters using multiple vanishing points. Combining these two methods (on the same perspective grid) will give you seamlessly integrated characters.

Materials
- *HB pencil*
- *ruler*
- *pen and ink*
- *colouring method of your choice*

Tip: Leave your vanishing point grid in the pencil art after designing any buildings or backgrounds so you can easily place any characters in the correct size and perspective.

1 Start with creating your two-point perspective grid from a horizon line drawn across the centre of your page. Add a stick figure or rough outline version of your character to capture the pose. If you draw a character's body connecting exactly with your perspective lines, it will look stiff and robotic. Use the grid to show which limbs should diminish into the background, and which thrown forward: the parts that should be drawn with foreshortening.

2 Now flesh out the character by creating the outline for the body, head and limbs, adding in muscle tissue to your chosen proportions. Use what you have learned about the action line and turning characters around three-dimensional axes to get your pose to work. Gain experience in figure drawing and you will find yourself using all these tools less. However, they are useful to fall back on whenever a posing problem presents itself.

3 After establishing the basic pose and shape of your character, you can start to pencil in the outfit they are wearing as well as any accessories, weapons or devices they might be holding or in the process of using. In this instance, our young warrior is wielding a sword in his far hand. Note how it is held low, pointing in a similar direction to his foot. See how the perspective affects the weapon in the same way as the arm that holds it.

4 When you are comfortable with your pencilled pose, ink over the lines and fill in your character. If you are drawing the character in isolation, you will want to erase the guidelines at this point and move to colour, as shown at right. If integrating your character into a background, use the existing perspective construction lines to ensure that your background lines up correctly with the figure.

Practice exercise: The character in a setting

Now to create a character in a setting, drawing the background first in three-point perspective and then adding in the figure using the same grid. Even though you will construct the background first, you should still sketch in some rough stick figures, to show where your characters will be situated. The view we'll use is a steep bird's eye view, with a character flying up towards us in front of our building. To ease the investment of time in the background we'll place the character close to the corner of a large building so you won't need to draw the detail of a street scene. Just as you are looking down on the building, so you will also be looking down on the character.

Materials
- *HB pencil*
- *ruler*
- *pen and ink*
- *colouring method of your choice*

1 Start with your three-point perspective grid, placing the horizon at the top of the drawing. Construct the large rectangular building as before, creating a grid from the third, low, vanishing point and the fanned guidelines from the two ends of the horizon line.

2 Add details to your building as before: windows in perspective, ledges, parapets, and so on. You could add shading to imply reflections in the glass. Keep these simple, so as not to distract from the character in the foreground. Sketch out the stick figure for this flying character's pose. Make him as big as you like, remembering foreshortening and perspective. His head and leading hand will be much larger than his body and feet, as they are closer to us.

3 Now construct your superhero in perspective, giving them more exaggerated muscle tone than a standard 'civilian' character. Here we are bringing his chibi-like head as close to the 'camera' as we can to make it loom large in relation to his body for a comedy effect. This superhero is wearing a Spandex outfit typical of this kind of character, and we have a cape operating in perspective as well. Don't forget to add details like a chest emblem and shoulder insignias to make your hero totally unique.

4 When you are happy with your lines, ink your character and the building and erase the extraneous guidelines, particularly the grid. When inking, pay close attention to your areas of solid shadow, which can add weight to your building and characters and help sell the illusion of depth. Figure out your main light source – if lit from above by the sun, the shadows will fall underneath the ledges and at the top of the windows. How would the same image look when lit from the street? Try out different lighting schemes.

Tip: If you have access to a lightbox, or are using paper thin enough to show up line work underneath, it may be helpful to create 'stock' perspective grids. They will save on drawing time and pencils. This method helps if using traditional colouring methods.

Present-day setting

If you want to set your story in the 'real world', your backdrop will naturally be the present day. This makes it one of the easiest settings to get to grips with. Becoming familiar with a couple of buildings will stand you in good stead when you design your own. Your understanding of perspective will be important in conveying the wider vision. Some artists don't enjoy backgrounds, preferring to concentrate on characters; but the background of your story is a character in its own right, its moods and interactions with your protagonists affecting them as much as – or more than – any human being.

Finding reference

Sources of reference can be taken from almost anywhere around you; from personal photographic reference of local buildings, or the use of Internet search engines to turn up pictures of far-flung locales. In order to get used to drawing a setting you might choose just a couple of buildings to study closely before you start to put them into your setting.

Photos from different angles ▶
Choose just a couple of buildings to study closely, photographing them from many different angles and making sketches of your results.

Creating buildings

One, two and three-point perspectives easily create basic geometric shapes. In constructing your own buildings, think about how you can use these shapes to create simple structures, like high-rise flats, essentially large obloid-shaped buildings. Unlike characters, there isn't really a 'manga' way of drawing buildings – the fact that manga spans such a large variety of genres and tastes means you have more than ample opportunity to put your own spin on the background environment.

Head office, head-on (near right) ▶
A standard obloid building, customized with asymmetrical window placements and an external lift at the left. This image is a plan view, with no perspective distortion.

Looking up (far right) ▶
This image is actually only in one-point perspective, as with the train tracks depicted earlier, but it does the job as well as a two or three-point image.

Creating a cityscape
When creating a cityscape, you can quickly create backdrops by using these obloids and adjusting their size.
As you build your confidence, you can complicate the structures, divide the storeys in different ways, adding residential balconies and colour detailing. Don't forget entrances: do the buildings have grand openings (pillars around the doorway and ostentatious canopies) or are they more subtle, or even run-down? Some areas of town are in better condition than others: how can you show the difference? Think about how to generate a downtrodden, disreputable block in a state of disrepair.

Beyond the city

When drawing an immediate area, think about how the city expands into the suburbs and beyond. Add distant buildings into background to create a greater sense of depth and a richer environment. Remember that the farther away an object or building is from the picture plane, the less detail will need to appear on it.

Motorway possibilities ▶

Storytelling options and destinations open up like exits on slip roads in this visual metaphor for a story's future.

Locations

Planning your locations with small, sketchy maps will help you keep track of your fictional locales. There's no need to map out your entire city, at least not until your imaginary setting becomes a runaway success and the call comes for tie-in tea merchandise, but for panel-to-panel continuity as your characters move, nothing beats an overview that allows you to accurately depict a street or block from any angle. Such maps can suggest storytelling possibilities or new angles that may not have occurred to you at the script stage. Keep them rough: they're for placement reference, not detail.

Tip: If you're looking for inspiration on layout, why not search for a map of your hometown on the Internet, or pick up a cheap driving map from your local bookstore? Both can quickly spark off endless municipal planning possibilities.

The plan ▲

The section of the street map shown above shows a town square, with a statue in the centre where six side streets converge. Surrounding the square are a number of buildings which could be shops or offices. The building closest to the statue could well be the town hall, the seat of government and first point of call for travelling adventurers. How tall are each of the buildings? What size are they? How many windows and doors do they have?

Facing the town hall ▲

Now that the plan is done you can sketch out your first shot. Here the statue of a lion commemorates the founding of the town, with the town hall immediately behind it and some of the surrounding buildings visible in the background. We can see the main streets continuing around the town hall on either side, as well as a side street on the left that suggests further possibilities for exploration.

Another view ▲

Now try to draw the same setting from a different angle. Instead of a close-up shot of the statue, this image uses it as the focal point of a long shot, showing the walk up one of the connecting city streets: perhaps the approach to the town hall from the town's heavily guarded gates. The buildings seem to fall away on the other side of the statue, and a wisp of blue on the horizon suggests the sea. Is this a coastal town?

Natural setting

The background in which you set your manga is a vital component of the story. It will not only aid the story's atmosphere and inform the reader exactly when and where the story takes place, but it can also reinforce your characters' emotions. This section will assist your illustration of common background elements, particularly the natural elements that surround us. It is worth remembering that research is the key element to getting a realistic situation right but that fine detail does not need to be provided if seen at a distance. This could save you a great deal of time when creating backgrounds.

Trees and vegetation

Natural settings live or die on the quality of their flora, so make sure you research or invent credible and appropriate vegetation. Trees and forests are an essential part of the outdoors, but each locale and country has its own varieties and species. Before drawing a forest in full, do a little research to get a sense of the basic shape of your chosen tree. Trees can add interest and vitality to densely packed urban areas, or a menacing, ageless quality to stories set out in the wild.

With little practice, you will be drawing them with ease. As with trees, the important part of drawing vegetation is to suggest the vegetation rather than define it. If pencilling an area of grass, add jagged borders where the turf meets the pavement, for example, as well as a few additional blades or tufts for texture. If digitally painting use rough strokes for the majority of your coloured areas, with a few points of detail for contrast.

Trees at midday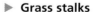
The midday sun throws these trees into even sharper relief, their foliage becoming a completely solid mass of colour, save for highlights at the tips. Radial lines from the sun cut into the treeline below.

▶ **Savannah trees**
Three roughly defined savannah trees are easy to distinguish in this example. A lighter-leaved tree is bookended by two darker-leaved siblings, each defined by blobby, speckled digital brushstrokes. Note that only the trunk in the extreme foreground is bounded by an outline; the others are pushed farther into the background by softer, unbounded colours. Gentle gradients define the land and grass; there is no need for detail at this distance.

▶ **Grass stalks**
Thick stalks of grass are suggested by overlapping lines in complementary and constrasting colours, shadows concentrated at the root, highlights at the tip. A few individualized stalks in the extreme foreground help frame the panel and 'fool' the brain into seeing the full amount of detail in every impressionistic stalk. This can save a great deal of time at the colouring stage. Outlined grass line art can be repeated and used again and again as a grassy texture.

Sunsets

The simple scattering of light particles in the atmosphere as the sun dips below the horizon alters, for a few short minutes, everything in its coruscating glow. Sunsets have a narrative component, too: suggesting the twilight of a story or relationship. As such, they can be a powerful addition to your storytelling toolbox. Sunsets shift along the visible light spectrum, from yellow to red to purple to blue, casting everything in your panel in a different value of that hue.

If working digitally, the simplest way to reproduce them is with a radial gradient, blending from yellow to red. Remember to work your chosen colours into your landscape and foliage, either as additional brush-strokes, or with a coloured filter over the entire image. In traditional media, cross-hatched colouring pencils or carefully blended watercolour paints can accomplish similar results.

◄ **Bold sunset**
This powerful sunset is communicated through colour rather than line work.

Setting the natural scene

For a natural setting you'll need to make sure you research the appropriate surroundings, so that you can be certain that you are putting your reader in the intended location for the story. In preparation of your setting you should look into doing some research into the sort of climate and country you're going to be writing about. Research will allow you to capture a more accurate portrayal of your landscape, as well as affect how detailed you are willing to allow your story to become. Check out the local flora, whether it is in the Amazonian Basin, the Gobi Desert or the English countryside. If buildings are to be placed in your natural setting you can do some general reference on different types of architecture that are suitable for the surroundings or find generic traits for certain types of buildings. You want the reader to believe in your world, so the less you give them to question, the more successfully the story will work in the way you want it to.

Far and close up view ▶
Both of these images are parts of the same whole. Your detailed research on the surroundings should be focused on whatever aspects of the environment you are intending to show.

Quasi-historical setting

Historical or quasi-historical settings in manga and anime do not automatically mean historically accurate. For example, the character in *The Ninja Scroll*, Jubei, is based on a figure said to have existed in Japan in the 18th century. While the traditional Japanese setting looks the part, the characters are often more than a little colourful, with elements of the supernatural added to the historical record. In *The Ninja Scroll*, Jubei faces an old adversary he once thought dead, who has aligned himself with several mysterious individuals, only one of whom seems to be a samurai. The others possess much stranger, even magical

gifts, each one increasing in relative power and ability as Jubei faces them, one by one. On top of their physical menace, Jubei is also striving to defeat a poison that is slowly killing him. From this example it can be seen that many liberties can be taken with history in order to produce a more exciting story – fiction is about entertainment, not history lessons. Because of the way older beliefs and stories so easily intertwine with actual historical eras, you will find that history and fantasy tend to mesh together well, particularly if pulled from 'existing' mythologies.

Practice exercise: Historical tale

The setting delves into the quasi-historical past for inspiration, mixing the flavour of the Tibetan monastery with the architecture of a more Greco-Roman style to produce a style that is at once authentic and fresh. In our tale, a group of monks head into the snowy peaks in search of a rare flower with fabled healing properties. Every novice undertakes this journey as a rite of passage, but this year's 'graduating class' will find their journey far more eventful than they believed possible. Consider: what religion do the monks belong to? How was the monastery constructed? What happens to the monks during their journey?

Materials
- *soft lead pencil*
- *pen and ink*
- *colouring method of your choice*

1 Here the monks ascend from their training halls at the foot of the mountain to the monastery itself, where they will be given directions on their mission. Although the jagged, natural outcrops and twisting hewn staircase complicate matters, there's only one vanishing point, at the top of the staircase. Keep your lines loose and sharp on the mountainside. Areas of light and shade are here delineated by colour. The monastery is made of two obloid shapes: use triangles to shape the roofs and Doric columns to add texture to the walls. Keep your figures in perspective, allowing them to diminish as they head up the steps to guide the reader's eye.

2 Now the monks have left the monastery, but have been forced to seek shelter in a cave after night falls and heavy snow descends with it. Using the same techniques as you used on the mountain previously, delineate the walls of the cave with areas of dark and light. Contrast the deep black of the night with the white pinpricks and flurried mounds of the snow. Use what you've learned about folds in clothing to successfully draw the monks' cloaks – and add the menacing shadow rearing over them using colour alone, laid on top of your line work.

3 Out of the darkness, as if condensing out of the squalls of snow, the shadow reveals itself as an Abominable Snowman: the Yeti. A figure of legend even in the world in which your story is set, will it prove to be the undoing of the monks? Or is it the gatekeeper of the fabled flower, the last test and guardian that the novices must pass without fear in order to become true monks? Perhaps the monks are so terrified they never lift their hoods, and the Yeti remains a legend. The Yeti is illustrated in a harsh black and white style, with only the faintest hint of colouring on its fur.

More quasi-historical settings

Here are just two brief examples of other ways in which you can blend a historical setting with a low-fantasy element to produce a highly original world in which to tell your stories. Using existing countries, eras and archetypes, but with a twist, can save you a lot of development time.

◀ **Civil War anti-hero**
Imagine a futuristic Cavalier and Roundhead clash in England. This armoured deserter is only after one thing: profit. Armed with a magic sword, he keeps being pulled into rescue missions against his will.

Spring-heeled Jack ▲
A lithe historical figure leaps across the rooftops striking fear into the city populace. Who will get to the bottom of the mystery?

Fantasy setting

A fantasy setting comes with the most creative freedom, because your ideas can be taken from anywhere, and incorporated in any form you see fit. Fantasy environments often incorporate architectural influences from all over the world, and you should adopt the same strategy. A broader knowledge of world architecture will give you an eye for combining them, altering them and springboarding from them to create new buildings of your own blended origin. Your hybrid setting will also influence the type of characters in them and their costumes, language, vehicles and animals.

Creating a fantasy setting

Towers are often associated with wizards and other hermit-like characters, and placed in locations that are difficult to reach, requiring great physical exertion to do so. Furthermore, the towers are littered with traps and built in extreme locations, where the elements themselves ward off visitors.

A meeting of worlds ▶
As an example, take the illustration of a tower shown here. This building uses a combination of English and Italian architecture to create a familiar but slightly 'off' look – fantasy thrives on a mixture of the familiar and the unearthly. The reference used to create it was from English churches and various old buildings that were photographed in Venice.

Climbing the staircase ▼
Farther down the tower, three young adventurers have braved the wastes to seek the Wizard's knowledge, and they are climbing one of the many steep staircases leading up to where they hope the Wizard is enthroned.

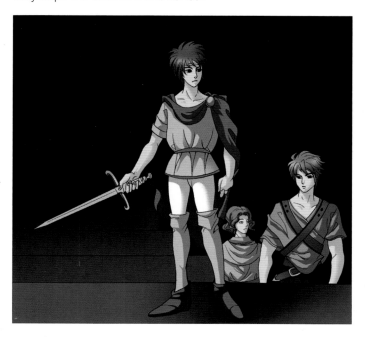

Relative scale ▼
Though the tower is large, we can show its dimensions more clearly by placing it in relation to its surroundings: here, the mountainous wastes of some long-forgotten tundra. Despite the size of the tower, the Wizard lives in cramped quarters at its summit, surrounded by papers, jars and curios.

A font of knowledge ▲
Wizards are known as accumulators of knowledge, both widely known and forbidden – scholars, possessors and, when threatened, wielders. Many adventurers come to them looking for wisdom, potions and guides, and many wizards will reward those hardy enough to make the journey – leaving the choice of how to use such knowledge in the hands of the wielder, passing on the burden of responsibility to a protagonist who must show themselves worthy.

Fantasy story

A tower is not just a background structure in such a fantasy story: it can also provide a structure for your story, each new level providing a new challenge for your heroes to overcome, with meeting the Wizard the ultimate aim and conclusion of your tale. Here is one possible magic trap found on the journey up the staircase: a strange sphere. Adventurers be warned: when visiting a Wizard, touch nothing!

Discovery ▲
This adventurer is brandishing the sphere, seemingly unaffected by it.

Transformation ▲
He is surrounded by a magical force that pulses through him.

Result ▲
Now a half-man/half-pig, the hero has an added impetus to find the Wizard and claim a counter-spell.

Practice exercise: Fantasy castle

Castles are fundamental to a classical fantasy setting. Many generic designs are based on medieval European fortresses, but, like the fantasy tower, it's entirely up to you which references and architectural schools you choose to amalgamate.

Materials
- *soft pencil*
- *pen and ink*
- *colouring method of your choice*

1 Use a two-point perspective to achieve a dramatic view of a typical castle interior. Draw your horizon line across the page, marking your vanishing points at either end of each line.

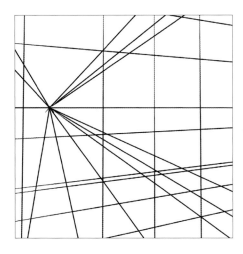

2 Next, draw out the fanned lines from each point to create your 3-D grid. Shade some of the lines to outline your room, adding in curved sections as where appropriate. The height of your vertical lines will be determined by where your ceiling is. You may want to add doors and rooms heading off from the main room.

4 Colour your work using your preferred method. Sometimes altering or twisting your perspective slightly can add a visual 'bounce' to your image and make it more interesting on the eye. Take your time with architecture, and don't get frustrated if your first results don't match your expectations.

3 Draw in any furniture (such as the chair of state shown here), wall mouldings, stonework, columns and so on. You may want to sketch them in as basic 3-D blocks to begin with, shaping the detail within them later. As with drawing people in perspective, in time you'll find you can draw furniture more or less freehand.

Cyberpunk setting

Most cyberpunk tales are set in a possible future where industry and technology have run to their logical and dystopian extremes. The majority are set on a near-future Earth, where cybernetic implants are common, a more advanced version of the Internet is seamlessly integrated with every aspect of everyday life, and where, for all its technological advances, society is still stricken by the same problems of poverty, crime, war and environmental disaster – all exacerbated by overpopulation and depleted natural resources. A cyberpunk setting is ideal for grim-and-gritty action-adventure stories, cautionary environmental fables about technology run rampant, or updated versions of noir detective stories with science fiction trappings. Style, body modification and cool technology are the bywords of cyberpunk. When it comes to your backgrounds, most stories take place in cramped, overbuilt and overcrowded city structures, ranging from crime-ridden slums of the lower classes to 500-floor skyscrapers of the privileged.

Overgrown city

When planning your cityscape, it may help to begin with an existing city and extrapolate 20 or 30 years' worth of building work on to it. Cram in more skyscrapers, joining the apartment and recreational blocks with tunnels and walkway systems hundreds of metres in the air. Perhaps hotels and office blocks now descend deep underground; perhaps the city's mass transport system is an inverted maglev railway slung between the buildings. Be creative with the manner in which development has run amok.

Urban jungle ▶
This illustration shows a street-level shot of a cyberpunk city slum. Life is eked out by drug-runners and cyber-tech peddlers at the feet of the wealthy apartment blocks. A mishmash of influences between East and West shapes the crammed-together billboards and rain-slicked shanty towns, as run-down flyers and second-hand mecha pass overhead.

Penthouse view ▶
Here we see the same city from the vantage point of wealth and familial excess. This city block is so tall it passes above the acid-rain clouds and allows a glimmer of smoggy sunlight to batter its UV-protected quadruple-glazed glass. Strut-like tunnels connect alternate floors of living accommodation with the buildings and transport hubs in the surrounding area, meaning that the super-rich can live their entire lives without breathing 'real' air or touching the ground.

Robots and cyborgs

One technological advance that has usually taken place is the proliferation of advanced robotics, artificial intelligence, and regularly used cybernetic implants which blur the line between human and robot. These robots can come in many shapes and sizes, from automated, sentient tanks to synthethic-skinned android duplicates that can perfectly mimic humans. It can be a common sight to see people with artificial eyes, arms and legs, all more powerful than the human norm. Some elements of your world may also pilot small-scale robotic combat suits – similar to the concept of mecha, but on a more personal scale. You may find the police equipped with four-armed walkers instead of cop cars, for example. Remember that these items will be available to the super-rich first – the lower rungs of society must make do with what they can steal or buy used.

▲ **Jet-pack police**
The skylines of this future city buzz with these red-and-purple enforcers of the peace. No one knows whether they are human, cyborg or fully robot underneath the helmet.

▲ **Armoured crime-busters**
Carbon fullerene armour enables these police to resist everything except a nuclear strike. Onboard fusion generators allow them to stay in the air for days at a time.

The super-computer

Another favoured trope of cyberpunk is the super-computer – an artificial intelligence, the Internet grown sentient, that controls everything. Cyberpunk is a child of the 1980s, so even with the increasing miniaturization of computer components, you'll still find cavernous rooms with cathedral-sized computers. Glimmering with flickering lights and extending cables like malevolent tendrils into every aspect of the city, few of these computer intelligences are benign. If such an intelligence forms the 'villain' of your story, the background and setting can transform themselves from mere set-dressing into a central character. An enormous computer towers over an insignificant human character; the latter has finally been surpassed. What has driven your intelligence to its evil ends? A glitch? A desire for self-preservation? A religious epiphany brought on by sentience, or a virus in the code? A desire to wipe out humanity in favour of android duplicates? The possibilities are endless.

▲ **Location as character**
This computer room threatens to become a tomb for the scientists working inside it, as the giant computer has decided that weak, human intelligences are not the best repositories for knowledge. Adapting its power cables into rudimentary digits, the system overwhelms one scientist and prepares to transfer his mind into its own data banks, storing data for all eternity within its mainframes. Of course, the process will rip their bodies apart, but that's a small price to pay for progress...

Steampunk setting

Steampunk is a quasi-historical 'sister-genre' to cyberpunk. It posits that all the technological advances known to the cyberpunk era – advanced robotics, artificial intelligence, body modification, and the like – occurred in a setting analogous to 19th-century England rather than the future. The setting draws inspiration from the inventor Charles Babbage's 'difference engine', an early steam-powered computer – thus, robotics and the like are all powered by complicated arrangements of steam-pistons or clockwork, rather than silicon. William Gibson and Bruce Sterling collaborated on the first modern novel using this premise, *The Difference Engine*,

with many other authors and artists following suit, drawing additional inspiration from the early science fiction novels such as Jules Verne's *The Time Machine*, Mary Shelley's *Frankenstein* and H.G. Wells' *War of the Worlds*. Steampunk tends to be a lot more optimistic and enlightened than cyberpunk about how progress can make the world better and more exciting at the same time. Manga has produced many tankobon (volumes) and anime in this genre, including *Steamboy* and *Laputa*, as well as the incredibly popular *Full Metal Alchemist* and a large majority of the *Final Fantasy* games and adaptations.

Steampunk locomotive

The quickest shortcut to creating a vibrant steampunk background is to shake up your carefully researched city streets and 19th century countryside with anachronistic, steam-based technology. Steampunk works best when viewing advanced technology of the present day through a filter of the past, translating burnished titanium, electrics and digital components for polished wood, brass and steam- or clock-driven elements. The locomotive created here follows these guidelines. The shape is solid rather than aerodynamic. This giant engine will keep on going, no matter what. Its shape was inspired by an old blacksmith's hammer. This locomotive has more substantial wheels than is traditional on account of its size.

◄ The rolling locomotive
The steam train resembles more of an ocean-going vessel than anything that travels on land, and, in our world, that's because the raw materials have been repurposed from the Victorian fleet. The locomotive's 'hull' has been specially reinforced and armoured to protect the engineers inside – as clockbot-assisted highwaymen often try to assault these landships as they make their vital journeys up and down the country. The pistons and wheels are similarly reinforced, and the funnels can be retracted and sealed to make the train an armoured refuge in a crisis.

Tip: Steampunk technology will tend to look far more ornate than the more quotidian devices of today. Mass-production is still in its infancy, and so each one of your steam-powered trains, power suits and flying machines will have been hand-crafted by a skilled artisan. Show some of these touches by adding sculptural and painterly flourishes in the wood and brass elements.

◄ Working the locomotive
From the side, the front of the unit is visible, protruding out from the head of the 'hammer'. How many steam engineers would be required to run such an engine, and what protective gear would they wear to deal with the immense heat produced by all that burning coal? What would the train's carriages look like? Research some 19th-century trains and see what you can come up with.

Steampunk vehicle

A moving, fully functioning vehicle can be the most fun to draw, as the best way to start is just to doodle your fantastic creation, bolting on parts as necessary until it fulfils your imagined function. Start with a boiler and smokestack, and develop from there.

Use a ramshackle, 'mad inventor' approach: leave as many workings visible as possible, and use reference of existing 19th and early 20th-century vehicles and buildings, taking visual elements and combining them in new and intriguing ways. For the vehicle

below, a combat infantry walker used in wartime, you would start with a basic barrel shape, and expand with a squashed hexagon, halved by the gun dome. The cogs and wheels visible on the side of the main body imply the logistics of the walking legs.

Combat infantry walker ▶
Providing the same support to infantry and cavalry as a fixed gun emplacement or tank, but with the flexibility of legs on rough or dug-in terrain. In *War of the Worlds*, Wells' invaders strode the countryside in giant tripodal walkers. Perhaps these devices are reverse-engineered from those, post-invasion. You could base other vehicles on old farming equipment or World War I tanks.

Steam-powered Gatling gun

Boiler venting stack

Pilot protected against steam scalds by goggles and boiler suit

Visible gears and clockwork

Swivelling ball-mounted cannon

Hinged steam-piston legs

Steampunk clockmakers

Tip: Think of the effort and precision required to create a clockwork robot with even half the functions of a silicon synthetic – and now imagine just how in demand these artisans would be. It would be enough to kill, die or go to war for. Your technology can often provide some excellent story hooks.

What would the buildings look like in your steampunk city? Think of 19th-century London, and all the factories there used to be; think also of famous, long-standing buildings. Clockwork mechanization is just as important as steam power to steampunk. Many businesses in the city would employ hydraulics specialists and former watchmakers, now elevated to cornerstones of your new society. The old watchmaker shown here has just finished re-rigging a broken alarm clock as a robot toy for his grandchildren. Our Geppetto-style creator has made a living thing from his livelihood. This clock is energized by stored potential energy, not magic.

◀ Make do and mend
Steampunk is all about the injection of fantasy into a historical period. This shows the contrast between quasi-historical elements like the old watchmaker, and fantastical elements, like the autonomous clockwork creation.

Interiors as backgrounds

Planning the décor, fittings and furniture for an interior scene is just as important as designing a full building and placing it in the context of a city. Many of your most important scenes will take place in interiors, and you have an excellent opportunity in every one of them to reflect character and amplify mood. A bare dockland warehouse has a very different feel to a boudoir strewn with voluptuous cushions, for example. If the room belongs to one of your characters, you should populate it with their personal effects. What do their favourite photographs, paintings and desktop wallpaper say about their personality and history? A minimalist or cluttered room can similarly speak volumes.

Aspects of a room

Unlike out on the street, where you may include a number of buildings in the background that have nothing to do with your story beyond scene-setting, every interior you show will be involved in the narrative somehow. As mentioned above, think how you can use the backgrounds of these scenes to drive your narrative. The old axiom of storytelling is 'show, don't tell', and a well-constructed interior scene can carry a great deal of weight and save you volumes of wasted panels and awkward dialogue. Treat every room like a reverse-engineered television murder scene: what will an investigator (the reader) be able to deduce from the props and trinkets in it? If you plan to use a room on a regular basis, don't forget to map it out so you can draw it from all angles.

Traditional Japanese meal ▲
The minimalist setting tells us the characters are concerned with people over property, and that the story is set in the past. The calligraphy on the table suggests an educated, perhaps noble, woman, as does the variety of the foods being eaten.

Room details

Manga's extensive page counts in most of its editions allows it to pace its stories in a different fashion to comics in the West. You may often find that manga takes the time to explore new surroundings, zooming in on pertinent details (either while characters continue talking, as a 'voiceover' on the characterless image, or as a guided 'walking tour' of a new locale) to create a sense of place. It also gives you, the artist, a chance to show off your research and planning, and draw the reader's eye to details that, while easily overlooked now, may become very important later. Don't feel you have to implement these 'breathing spaces' in the narrative every time you move somewhere new – like every storytelling technique, they should be used as appropriate and in moderation.

The calligraphy table ▼
Drawing attention to the roll of paper, ink and pen might just seem like adding detail on first glance, but perhaps the noblewoman is writing a message to her lover that she is desperate to keep her husband from reading.

Starting off

The simplest place to start when deciding on décor is to look at familiar surroundings, like your bedroom or lounge. Take note of how you've decorated your room: where you've placed the bed, the bedside cabinet, bookcases, lamps, wardrobe, chest of drawers and so on. What smaller, personal details have you placed on these pieces of furniture? Draw your room from one perspective, then focus on a few chosen pieces of furniture and draw them from as many angles as you can. Learn the shapes they're made from, and practise drawing them in one, two and three point perspectives. This will give you an 'image bank' of common furniture to draw from.

Making it personal

If your central character works out of an office, what does their workstation look like? If they work in a cubicle farm full of hundreds of identical workstations, how could you tell that it was your protagonist's desk without them being there? Thinking of these unconscious clues and physical remnants will often give you a better handle on your character's personality. Add personal details that give up more information on a second glance – the photo of a friend, pet or lover stuck to the monitor, sticky notes and 'to-do' lists on the wall. A mishmash of papers 'perfectly filed' according to your character's own peculiar system (which works only for them), and an in-tray stuffed with ignored memos.

◄ **Manga artist's desk**
Even without the artist present, the morass of pencils and pens, drying sketches, freelance commissions and thumbnail sketches would give him or her away.

Furnishing the fantasy setting

A fantasy setting has a similarly rich variety of furniture and personal items, although it is harder to research them by just looking in your bedroom. The interiors of castles, alchemists' labs, fletchers (makers and sellers of bows and arrows) and taverns would all have their own items. Though the traditional medieval-sourced fantasy worlds do allow you plenty of scope for research, you might want to add your own stamp to your creations. The tip here is consistency. Tables, chairs, beds and other furniture should be linked by style, particularly in rich areas like castles or the mountain homes of creepy noblemen. If tables are black mahogany, chiselled with gargoyle heads, then chairs and sideboards should match. In poorer hovels, consistency goes out the window: the people who lived in poorer homes would own whatever was affordable, available, or built by their own hands.

Fantasy interior ▲
Here is the grand entrance hall to a nobleman's weekend retreat. Far from the serfs tilling the fields that swell his coffers, he and his fellow socialites swill the finest wines – and then, when the witching hour arrives, they descend to the basement for a frenzy of demonic sacrifice. How would you decorate and furnish such a room and such a house? The chessboard tiles on the floor already illustrate the dichotomy of good and evil within the house – how would the chairs and tables reflect the same internal struggle?

Versatile vehicles

Vehicles are present in every kind of story. The examples shown here are cars, but the principles used to draw them can be extended to the hovercar, the horse-drawn cart and beyond. Vehicles are essential elements of your story in three ways: as set-dressing material, adding fizz and visual interest to street scenes; as backdrops, as characters converse behind the wheel or make out on the back seat; and as characters in their own right, extensions of personality. As with feet, it's hard to cheat a drawing of a car and make it look good – so brush up on the basics.

Practice exercise: Basic car shape

Cars are basically boxes on wheels, but it's the intersection of the various angles that can prove tricky to draw.

1 Draw two loose rectangles, one on top of the other. The upper one is drawn shorter than the other and placed slightly aft of centre above the lower one, with its sides tilting inwards in a trapezoidal fashion. Draw two circles at either end of the lower rectangle, bisected by the chassis and leaving space for the bumpers at front and rear. This forms the basis of an exceptionally simple car frame. You should be able to rotate this shape in any direction or dimension.

Materials
- *soft lead pencil*
- *pen and ink*
- *colouring method of your choice*

2 Using the basic frame, begin to 'cut into' the squared-off shapes with pencil lines, carving out the more rounded contours of modern car bodywork. Have a look at some photo reference (or a real car) to see how the chassis curves over the wheels, where the windows and doors fall, and how bumpers and headlights are incorporated.

3 Each car begins with this basic frame, but obviously every model and make is a slightly different variation on the 'four wheels and an engine' frame. When you are happy with how your car looks (not forgetting details such as wing mirrors, grilles, licence plates, hubcaps, door handles and trim), ink the lines and prepare your drawing for colour. When colouring, pay particular attention to how the metal panels reflect and refract light, and how that reflection differs from the glare of sun or streetlights on the windscreen glass. Remember that a car's bodywork may pick up mud or road debris.

Practice exercise: Typical saloon car

The next example uses the same frame to construct a modern saloon car. Cars often have 'faces' formed by their headlight, grille and licence plate combinations. Here, the buck-toothed basic car above is outdone by the confident grin on this saloon. How does ` this reflect the owner's personality?

Materials
- *soft lead pencil*
- *pen and ink*
- *colouring method of your choice*

1 Even a slight change in proportion is enough to set the saloon car apart. The wheels are relatively larger, the chassis shallower and the windscreen swept back.

2 Add in the detail work, concentrating on the grille, headlights and wheeltrims. Ink your favoured lines, and erase your guidelines and bounding boxes if you have not already done so.

3 As before, pay particular attention at the colouring stage to the way light falls on the car's bodywork. The car here has been completely toned in a narrow range of blues, bleeding from dark to near-white for the highlights. Note how the highlights serve to pick out the angles of the car, separating the right wheelmount from the bonnet and leading the eye back along the doors to the boot.

Practice exercise: High-performance car

Although saloons and ten-a-penny basic cars are excellent for background and 'extras' work, you may want something with a little more oomph for your protagonist. High-performance cars are often squatter and wider than normal cars, and decked out in all kinds of extra spoilers, lights, visible engine blocks and the like. A character driving one of these cars is usually in far too much of a world-saving hurry to worry about such niceties as speed limits or traffic laws... So beware!

Materials
- *soft lead pencil*
- *pen and ink*
- *colouring method of your choice*

1 Flatten and widen your guide boxes. Manga characters will often drive something customized and unique, so combine a number of reference pictures to make your mean machine. This car combines 'billion dollar sports car' with 'Formula One racer' and adds in a dash of futuristic hovercraft. Use angles, shapes and colours not normally seen on the road.

Tip: Think about how much colour alters our perception of cars – flame red is seen as 'fast', with gunmetal grey being one of the more common colours on the roads. What does your character's car colour say about them?

2 This car has a swept-forward 'nose cone' for a bonnet, with the headlights and air-coolant feeder systems arranged around it over the wheel hubs. Add the larger shapes in first, such as the windscreen, wheels and door. Sketch in the fins and wheeltrims, sunken headlights and wing mirrors next. Many high-performance cars have two doors instead of four, the back seats having been removed to reduce the chassis weight and allow more room for a turbo-charged engine and stabilizing fins in the rear.

3 The tyres of a sports car are usually bigger than normal to allow for greater speeds while maintaining grip. Some models also have vents, intakes and spoilers to increase airflow and reduce air resistance. Spoilers increase downforce on the car, keeping the weight evenly distributed and the car under control at high speeds. When your chosen combination of speed, power and grace is complete, ink the pencil lines and erase your guide boxes. Finally, colour the whole vehicle in a hot red shade, using contrasting cool blues for the glass. If your character is a superhero or member of a police force or mecha gestalt, you may want to apply a suitable logo to the top of the bonnet, so enemies will know from a distance who is speeding to defeat them.

Multi-purpose planes

Planes are as flexible as cars in their in-story use. If a crime thriller is set in an airport, they could just be background scenery, or the location of a gripping terrorist shoot-out. If your characters are travelling from country to country, they could be present solely in an intermission panel to show how they crossed the distance. If your story is about a group of fighter pilots, however, the planes could be as individual and personable as the humans flying them. A fighter squadron gives you plenty of story opportunities, from ground-based drama to vicious dogfights, so here we'll show you how to draw a jet fighter, for use as a vehicular character or set-dressing for dramatic fighter-base brawls.

Practice exercise: Jet fighter

This jet fighter is drawn in a simple two-point perspective just below the horizon. Photo references for jet fighters are easy to come by, whether on the Internet, or through books like the *Jane's* series of guides.

Materials
- *soft lead pencil*
- *pen and ink*
- *colouring method of your choice*

> **Tip:** If one of your vanishing points isn't visible on the paper size you are using, you can 'cheat'. Either choose the true point (off the edge of your paper) and rule lines from that, or stay on the paper and make the lines taper together a little as they head off the page.

1 Draw your 'distance' vanishing point and draw perspective lines from it to construct the fighter's fuselage. Add in construction lines from the second vanishing point (off the page) to create construction lines for the wings.

2 Sketch in a pointed oval to represent the nose cone of the fighter, and begin shaping the slightly boxy dimensions of the fuselage, which diminishes back towards the 'distance' vanishing point.

3 Now add in the cockpit (as another pinched oval), and the slung-back wings, which jut out at an angle from the boxy main body of the fighter. Add the tailplanes behind them, underlapping the wings. Note that both the wings and tailplanes are 'squared off' at the tips, again at an angle.

4 At this stage, add the jet intakes either side of the cockpit as two more rectangular shapes, and the jet engine outlets as sawn-off ovals between the tailplanes. Sketch in the upright tailfins at a 45-degree angle to the tailplanes you have already drawn. Finally, sling two missile payloads under the wings.

5 Check that all of the elements in your fighter are working to the correct perspective, and begin to add some more surface detail – from the struts supporting the glass of the canopy to the metal seams that run along the fuselage, engines and nose cone. When you are happy with your details, ink them and erase the pencils.

Engines

Jet intakes

Cockpit and canopy

Telemetry package in nose cone

Weapons payload

6 Like the saloon car on the previous spread, this jet has also been coloured using a minimalist colour scheme – in this case a tight range of blue-silvers. Remember that planes are usually painted to match their combat theatre, so marine fighters will be painted sea-blue on top and sky-white underneath, or in various shades of grey. Desert operations fighters will come in tan and sandy hues, and jungle-bound jets will have green camouflage patterning.

Tip: Just as steampunk devices reuse existing 19th-century designs, there's no reason why you can't adapt modern-day tech for a near-future storyline. How could a jet fighter be adapted for space conflict against an alien race? What advances in engine technology would need to be made – or stolen?

Populating the skies

Of course, it's not just jet fighters that fill up airports and swoop through the skies; there are a huge variety of flying machines active in the modern era, and many more which have long gone out of use or never flown, except in the imagination. If working primarily in present-day stories, familiarize yourself with the technology that's out there, and the many different forms that it takes. If working in a future or parallel setting, try fusing different shapes and technologies into strange but familiar fuselages and aerodynamic transports. The helicopter and commercial airliner shown here are equally great for foreground or background use.

High-spec helicopter ▼
A lithe, radar-lite shape; fold-out gun and missile emplacements; side-mounted winch mechanisms; and a large field of view for both pilots and soldiers – this helicopter is used in anti-submarine warfare.

Tail rotor system

Main rotor

Cabin

Landing gear

Commercial liner ▶
Built for relative comfort, long-haul flights and the maximum number of civilian passengers, such planes, the lifeblood of most airports, are built for sturdiness, rapid turnaround times and minimal maintenance.

Vertical stabilizer

Cockpit

Engines

Fantasy setting project

One thing common to all settings is a drinking establishment. Whether it's a seedy dive for uncovering information in exchange for money or beatings, or a place to unwind at the end of a long day of asteroid mining, pubs and drinking dens always make for a fun and useful addition to any story. Look at the cantina in *Star Wars: A New Hope*, for instance: a showcase for dozens of aliens (who never appear again), but an important fulcrum for the whole saga and a hyper-condensed blast of science fiction flavour. For this project, we'll create a fantasy pub. As with your town square or starship deck, it's worthwhile drawing out a floor plan of your drinking hole so that you know where all the angles are when a bar room brawl kicks off. Think of the pub called 'The Prancing Pony' in *The Fellowship of the Ring* as an example. It has a main bar and seating area on the ground floor, with nooks and crannies for private meetings. Upstairs there are rooms to stay in, below are cellars where ale, wine and mead are kept. Give your tavern an 'Olde Pub' name, raising reader expectations with a foreboding moniker like 'The Bloodied Badger' or 'The Palcied Elf', or offer hope for sanctuary or entertainment with a sign reading 'The Merry Druid' or 'The Lusty Dwarf'.

Materials
- *soft lead pencil*
- *pen and ink*
- *colouring method of your choice*

◀ The centrepiece of our pub is the bar at the far end of the room where the ogreish landlord dispenses large tankards of frothy ale to all manner of clientele.

1 Start by mapping out a floor plan of your drinking establishment. Work out what the focal point of your pub is (the bar, a raised stage area for bardic entertainments) and arrange the furniture so that it complements and faces this focal point. Stairs on the far side lead down to the cellar, while visitors are politely asked to store their armour and weapons in the lockers close to the door.

stairs to cellar   window

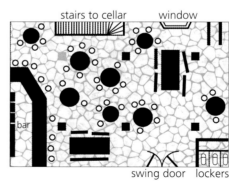

bar

swing door   lockers

2 Once you've planned your building, pick an interesting angle from which to draw your first shot. We've chosen a front-on view of the far right end of the bar, with two tables and a selection of stools jutting into shot, the better to show off the flavour and varied clientele of our pub.

3 We start by transposing the furniture and background from our top-down plan into three dimensions. The image uses a simple one-point perspective. Once you're happy with the placement and size of your backdrop, it's time to add in your merry drinkers, who can come in all shapes and sizes: the fiercesome dwarf in a helmet and the cocky elfin-like character are both in attendance at the pub on this occasion.

4 The final tavern scene has the green-skinned landlord standing behind the bar, visible from the torso upwards, talking to and serving his bizarre clientele. The loud hustle and bustle of his patrons fills the room, as talking weasels discuss bounties with zombie girls, and wall-eyed blue ghouls clank tankards with pigoblins. Behind the landlord, various barrels, glasses, bottles, wanted notices and old pub bric-a-brac fill out the décor, giving it a familiar, even cosy feel at odds with the strangeness of the customers. The warm earth tones of the walls, barrels and floor contribute to this sense of frontier security.

The characters

The first patron is a dwarf, short on stature, long on beard. The character's proportions are similar to a super-deformed version of a full-sized human, though they maintain the high level of detail in this instance. Emotions will mainly be communicated by the eyes, as the beard, helmet and armour cover up everything else. Physical actions will need to be exaggerated when drawn, to claw back the 'height advantage'.

The second patron has an almost dog-like quality to his elven head. Use standard human proportions and drawing methods when constructing him, but add a canine kink to the nose, jaw and teeth, and elongate the ears and limbs. This character relies on his own tough skin to see him through a fight, so show his cockiness by dressing him mostly in work-out bandages and cutting back on his clothing.

The ogreish landlord shown here has given up preying on the innocent to prey on those who can keep him in a ready supply of gold, in return for goblin intoxicants. He's another character with almost super-deformed proportions, loose muscle mass, and inhuman bone structure allowing him to support bizarre allocations of fat. Note the black, dead eyes and the two-fingered hand.

Spacecraft project

Spacecraft are another form of vehicle with multiple uses. Some, like the project here, are so large they could form the entire setting for your story, taking over a day to walk their length. Others are equivalent to the jet fighters we have already drawn, and are often mounted inside such enormous spacecraft like fighters on an aircraft carrier. Because these immense structures, thousands of metres long, are built in space and designed never to land, there are no design constraints on what they look like or what type of metal they are built out of. In the vast vacuum of space, there's no need for aerodynamic proportions. Anything goes, from the bulky and workaday to the artistic, abstract and awe-inspiring. This project will create the ultimate setting and transport for your science-fiction characters.

Materials
- *soft lead pencil*
- *pen and ink*
- *colouring method of your choice*

Engines

Main bridge

1 Start with the outside of the ship and work inwards. Sketch some thumbnail designs, incorporating your own ideas and your references. If you like multiple ideas, save your 'cast-offs' for other spacecraft in your interstellar fleet. When you're happy with a thumbnail design, sketch it out as an enlargement from multiple angles and perspectives, then ink and colour it.

Tip: When collating reference for the outer hull of the ship, look far and wide. Think about aircraft carriers and submarines, office blocks and cathedrals; anything with a large spatial area and an intriguing look or silhouette.

2 When the exterior of your ship is complete, create a cutaway diagram like the one shown at left and design a floor plan, giving you an idea of where each of the main rooms is located on your craft, what their functions are, and where they are located in relation to the rest of the craft. A detailed schematic will greatly help you at the story-planning stage, when working out where to stage certain scenes, and how to move characters through the ship. If you finish them to a high enough standard, you could even incorporate the floor plans into your story, as schematics to be stolen or imagery to flash up on the internal monitors. You could even give them to the reader as a complete map, extra information interspersed between chapters of the actual story.

Viewscreen data ▲

Embellish your bridge (and all the corridors and rooms of your ship) with symbols, signs and operating data terminals. Make 'working' rooms look as if they are being used, rather than leaving them as empty shells for characters to talk over and walk through on the way to somewhere else.

The bridge ▲

Central command hub for the entire ship, buried deep inside the hull. Being well defended makes it easier to resist an enemy's attempts to kill the bridge crew. All shipboard decisions are routed through here.

Tip: Try to continue your design decisions from the exterior of the ship through to the inside. A cathedral-inspired ship could be filled with giant atriums flooded with artificial light, while one based on a submarine might incorporate tight, duct- and pipe-filled tunnels. How would you combine these two influences on one ship? Perhaps the atria are there to stave off space-claustrophobia brought on by a life lived in pipes.

Space periscope ▶

Think about how each area of the ship or bridge may be used, and the items of technology required in them. This scanning terminal allows an operative to sweep deep space for visuals.

3 Choose a central room to illustrate in more detail. Here we've chosen the bridge, the hub of the ship. This is assembled in much the same way as any other room – start with a floor plan, decide on a style of furniture and any design motifs you will carry through the piece, and transfer the room into three dimensions. Here, the motif is angled geometric shapes and soft purples and browns. The focus of the room is on the giant viewscreens, with the crew seated on the inertial-dampening couches during flight.

4 When your bridge shot is complete, think of how you will use it during a story. Which angles will prove most dramatic? If the Captain is in an elevated position, try drawing her seat from below the horizon line, so that the reader – and the Captain's subordinates – are always looking up at her. If your characters are always seated in flight, which new angles can you find on your 'set' to keep things exciting and moving when they are largely stationary working at their stations or talking for hours on end?

Allies and enemies

Your manga heroes and the stories you create for them are only as good as the secondary characters you surround them with. This chapter will show you how to populate your narratives with intriguing and memorable people, animals and sentient vehicles: everything from friendly furry pets and loyal hounds to nefarious master thieves and city-block-sized mecha, the pilot-controlled walking vehicles.

Animal allies

Animals can be used in various ways. They can 'dress' a scene as background elements, or they can be used anthropomorphically, i.e. given human features and characteristics. An anthropomorphized animal may walk upright, talk, wear glasses and enjoy drinking coffee, for example. Animals can also be included as allies to a protagonist, particularly in shonen manga, where they are often 'familiars' – an extra set of eyes and ears for the main character. Such familiars, following a long tradition of Japanese spirit guides, often have the ability to talk and sometimes possess magical abilities.

Whether allies or not, animals in manga are frequently employed as a source of humour. An animal can be used to alleviate a heavy emotional juncture in a story with a moment of amusement. An animal's folly may also sometimes result in the discovery of something that will assist the main character.

Practice exercise: Cute cat, three-quarter view

In this exercise, you will be drawing a cute, manga-style cat. As in the earlier exercises on drawing human heads, you need to draw guidelines first, to ensure the cat's features are symmetrical.

Materials
- *soft lead pencil*
- *ink and pen*
- *colouring method of your choice*

1 Use a squashed sphere as your basic head shape. Imagine it as a three-dimensional shape, like a rugby ball, and make your guidelines follow the shape's curvature, as shown here. Lightly sketch in circular guides for the ears. For the body, draw two overlapping spheres below the head. The first (forelegs) sphere should be one head high. The hindlegs sphere should be one-and-a-half heads high. For the tail, draw three overlapping oval shapes as shown with a curved line at the end. Add points to the ear guides and to the cheeks. Use your body guides to sketch the length of the front and back legs, using straight lines to indicate limbs and ovals for feet.

2 Add in the cat's eyes, which are almost triangular in shape, using your guidelines to keep them evenly spaced in perspective. Although cats' pupils are almond-shaped, a 'cute' cat will have more circular pupils. Beneath the triangular button of the nose, add a loose 'UU' shape for the mouth, and stroke out six lines for the whiskers.

3 Start to join up and fill out your sketched lines, linking the outer edges of the head, drawing the inner ears, a pair of intrigued eyebrows, and joining the jawline to the pointed fur on the cheeks. Fill out the legs, and suggest paws with small arcs on the feet. Add fur to the tail with a jagged edge. Add a large bow as the final step.

4 Ink your pencil lines. When you are happy with your black and white drawing, add colour using your preferred method. Markers or watercolour paints will give you a soft and natural finish, while digital colours, as shown in this finished piece, will provide bold contrasts.

Practice exercise: Cute cat, side view

In this exercise, you will draw the same cat from the side, illustrating how the same basic building blocks – curved guidelines around a three-dimensional oval – can be used to capture the cat's features from any angle.

Materials
- *soft lead pencil*
- *pen and ink*
- *colouring method of your choice*

1 Draw a squashed sphere for the head, narrower than the one in the previous exercise. Remember that the facial features need to shift 90 degrees to the right.

2 As before, draw two guides for the body, placing the upper sphere under the head and the larger sphere trailing away from the small one. Don't forget the tail and ears.

3 Rough in your pencil lines as before, taking into account the portions of the cat that will be hidden or diminished by perspective. Note how the shapes of the eye, ear and cheek change when seen from the side.

4 When you are satisfied with the pencil lines, ink in the lines using your preferred method. Continue to take into account the way the proportions appear to change when viewed from this new angle – the size of the back leg or the whiskers, for instance. Erase your guidelines and colour the picture as before.

Contrasting characters

Cute mouse ▼
A mouse with a more anthropomorphized face. The cheeks and nose are minimalized, and the eyes separated. A tuft of 'hair' on the top of the head, and some eyebrows, humanize this creature even further.

Mean mouse ▲
To create a mouse make the ears round rather than pointy and perform the same rounding-off on the cheeks. Give the mouth protruding buck teeth. Make the feet shorter and the tail long and thin. The nose should be much larger in proportion to the rest of the face.

Cute bunny ▲
The head is the same shape as the mouse's but the ears are long, even stretched upwards. There is only a touch of furriness around the cheeks, with jagged lines kept to a minimum. The feet are long and the tail a small ball of fuzziness.

Mean bunny ▼
It takes only a few quick strokes to create an 'anti' version of a cute rabbit character, the mean bunny. Narrow the eyes and rotate them upwards, adding strong, lowered eyebrows to help insinuate a frown. Add a threatening pair of over-long, sharp gnawing teeth. Enlarge the paws and exaggerate the feet to kicking size. When drawing the fur, make the jagged edges longer and more pointed, to give a wilder appearance. The fighter's sash completes the look.

Realistic animals

Manga also uses more realistic-looking animals in a wide variety of naturalistic poses. These animals rarely stay still, so change their poses frequently. To get a better idea of how animals look in motion, study wildlife documentaries

or do some research into animal physiology at the library or on the Internet. This will provide you with a wide range of reference material from which to draw accurate information and inspiration.

White wolf ▼
This enormous wolf regards your characters with lupine intelligence. Will it guide them safely through the Arctic wastes – or rip out their throats?

Black bear ▶
Just woken from hibernation, this creature has more than freshwater fish or picnic baskets in mind for its first meal. The bloodshot eye and exaggerated fur underscore its role in your story as a predator.

Practice exercise: Realistic dog, standing

In this exercise, the realistic dog is drawn standing still, although its muscles are tensed and it is ready to chase after the nearest small rodent

or delicious treat. Take note of how the legs are arranged in front and behind the trunk of the body to better show the perspective.

Materials
- *soft lead pencil*
- *pen and ink*
- *colouring method of your choice*

1 Draw two ovals for the chest and rump. Join them as shown. Add a rough circle and triangle for the head and muzzle. Rough in the legs, taking note of how the knees bend and how each tapers to a paw. Sketch in the tail.

3 If completing your drawing as a pencilled piece, use photo reference or the image to shade in areas of muscle mass and shadow, suggesting fur and a tightly coiled, racing-dog frame. Tensed sinews will show themselves as light parallel lines along each leg.

2 Using these shapes as a guide, draw in the outlines of the body, adding in muscular detail and elements such as the ears, eyes and nose. Pay special attention to the leg muscles and paws.

4 Alternatively, you may wish to colour your dog. In this case, use colour rather than shading to suggest its musculature.

Practice exercise: Realistic dog, running

This exercise features a side view of a running dog. The lines representing the leg bones are pushed out beneath the snout and tail, creating a long, bullet-like silhouette.

Materials
- *soft lead pencil*
- *pen and ink*
- *colouring method of your choice*

1 Using much the same basic skeleton as in the last exercise, draw in the two ovals and connecting tissue for the body, and extended ovals for the head and tail. Draw the dog's four legs fully extended, flung out to front and back.

2 Add the paws and the details to the head such as the ears and the mouth (dogs tend to run with their mouths open) and make refinements to the shape of the body. Note the way the knees bend at the extremes of motion.

3 Draw the eye as a small almond shape at the point on the eyeline where the forehead ridge meets the snout. Firm up the sketchy lines from the previous step, streamlining the anatomy and inking your pencil lines when you are happy with the position of the limbs and the texture of the fur.

4 Go over your dog's outline and add jagged fur lines on the tail, chest, around the collar in ink (following the curve of the head circle), across the lower body, the back, and the tail. Remove the guides and add paws and a lolling tongue. Add colour, without losing the detail of your fur lines.

Other dog characters

Here are three different dogs, all of which use the same underlying skeleton bent into different poses and overlaid with different musculature. The resulting form is then accentuated with different sub-species traits.

Droopy dog ▼
Old and wise in dog years, or panting for water in the heat? The droopy jowls do much to add character.

Fierce dog ▶
A studded chain, blackened eyes, sharp claws and obstinate, jowly face show a dog not to be messed with.

Watchdog ▶
The pricked ears and 'battle-ready' stance reveal an alert watchdog on the prowl.

Tip: You can apply many human character traits to dog physiology to produce the same effects – excess fat suggests a lazy dog, muscle mass a fighter, long and lithe limbs a runner, and so on.

Animal monsters

Monstrous animals are not hard to develop once you have got to grips with the basics of animal drawing. Making something look demonic and threatening is just a matter of exaggerating certain features or fusing multiple species together to create a new gestalt entity. For inspiration, and in keeping with manga's roots, why not delve into some Japanese folklore? You will find hundreds of fascinating monsters and demons in all shapes and incarnations to choose from.

Mixing the gene pool

Monsters can be made by combining the attributes of one species with another – a trick that has kept mythological tales going for centuries. For example, a minotaur takes the form of a muscular man to the neck, but has the head of a ferocious bull. Don't feel you have to confine yourself to two species, either: some of the most memorable monsters of legend are fusions of wildly different arms of the zoological record. Depending on whether your monster is supposed to be 'realistic' (i.e. plausible) or not, you may wish to limit its strangeness to the boundaries of extreme possibility, or you may want to go with a fantastical mix of feathers and claws, manes and fur.

Blue Leo-Bull ▲
Fusing the raw attributes of the king of the savannah with the furious temper and horns of a bull, this blue-furred monster operates best in sub-zero wastelands.

Eagleman scout ▲
Living in vertiginous city-states clinging to the tips of mountains, Eaglemen eke out a primitive existence, stealing from those who dare cross their territories and bringing what they take as offerings before their twin-beaked god.

Taurean chieftain ▲
One of the leaders of a race of humanoid bull-men, vicious defenders of nature.

Hippohorse warrior ▲
This gene-splicing has sacrificed fleetness of foot for thick muscle and girth.

Practice exercise: Hellhound

In this exercise, an ordinary dog is made monstrous. The key is in how you alter its build. This dog does not have an athletic physique, with its fat body and sinewy legs. It is an ugly beast with some surprising features. It will also need far less hair – a few tufts on its back and behind the front legs, perhaps a few straggly bits on the tail if you choose, but no more.

Materials
- *soft lead pencil*
- *pen and ink*
- *colouring method of your choice*

1 Using the proportions of the realistic dog as a template, form the body shape using the same guide lines and joints for the legs, as well as the circle for the head and the rectangular muzzle. Elongate all of the proportions, from the spine to the yawning lower jaw, keeping your lines tight to the bone to show how the muscle has all but wasted away. The paws are now more like hideous claws.

2 Hang the jaw open and ready to reveal racks of prominent teeth, and position the nose. Bulk up the muscles of the neck by making the back arch farther away from the upper body. This will give the creature a hunched or razor-backed look. Add bony protrusions, such as the horn-like spar protruding from the forehead, to suggest hellish mutations and deranged cross-breeding experiments. Add manacles to the front claws, restraining the hellhound's aggression, but not completely denying the beast its freedom.

3 Draw in the details of the hellhound implying a deranged, possessive owner. Add piercings to the ears. Draw the eyes as demonic slits, burning with hatred. The hellhound can take all the damage you throw at it and still be aggressive so make the creature's skin look patchy and flayed, even slashed open in parts to show organs or muscle tissue, such as in the stomach. Fill in the deadly maw of jagged teeth and the hot, panting tongue. Add striations to the horn and claws and jagged fur to the whiplike tail. Ink the image when done, and erase the pencil lines.

4 The final stage adds colour. Fiery, earthen tones add credence to your impossible creation, with highlights of blood-red eyes and stomach, bone white teeth, and the contrast of the claws. The blues of the chains and piercings on the ears draw attention to the metal, contrasting sharply with the darker muted tones of the hellhound itself, which is a mixture of browns, pinks and reds, which indicates the poor condition of its skin.

Alien life forms

Aliens can be a lot of fun, as you can populate entire worlds with stunning new species. Aliens don't have to be a life form you'd ordinarily recognize. Even if humanoid, their characteristics may be based on completely different organisms. Alternatively, your aliens may look completely bizarre – take the creature from *The Blob*, for example: a roaming gelatinous mass. Once you've decided your aliens' physiology, you can develop interesting traits for them, which may similarly challenge convention. If you make your aliens drooling, snarling and generally threatening in appearance, that doesn't mean they have to be warmongering megalomaniacs. They could be peace-loving, with external features that make other races too afraid to have any sort of contact with them. Alternatively, you could develop an alien that appears serene, but which uses its calm exterior to lure others into a false sense of security.

Insects and reptiles

Here are some ideas for alien characters based on various existing Earth species. The first is a melding of ant, lion and dragonfly. The second is a fusion of earthworm, scorpion and octopus. The third is a blending of bat, dog and horse. All share an upright, humanoid gait. These alien forms have been inspired by insects, mammals and reptiles. Because the physiology of animals is so different from our own, combining their attributes always provides fertile ground for interesting ideas. Species such as ants and termites, for instance, live in hive-like colonies of workers dominated by a single queen, so creating alien societies based on these creatures could extend into their social practices within your story, sparking off potential ideas for thrilling interspecies conflicts.

Dragantflion ▲
No more than 15cm (6in) tall, dragantflions are the most brutal hunters in their food chain, swarming on victims with the use of pheromonal hive signals. Don't just cut and paste your animal attributes, think of how you can convincingly meld together elements that would never arise in nature.

Wormoction ▲
Caught between claws and squirting ink, a wormoction's prey never has a chance. Sometimes adding in pseudo-mechanical elements can add an extra element of the alien to your created species. Here, visible joints suggest an exoskeleton, or perhaps even naturally occurring hinges.

Bathorschien ▲
These monstrous-looking beings are simply misunderstood. On their holy days, thousands fill the skies with song. Think of surface textures for different alien skins. Applying fur instead of scales, or changing the colour of an Earth-based dermal covering can be enough to convince.

Practice exercise: Mantoid

The armoured mantoid, a soldier of a man/ant race, is naturally well-suited to battle. Its segmented limbs and anthead make it look sufficiently alien, while its humanoid body could allow it to blend in on Earth – just.

Materials
- *blue pencil 10*
- *soft lead pencil*
- *pen and ink*
- *colouring method of your choice*

1 Start with a rough outline with the blue pencil, building on what you have learned of human proportions. Use guidelines if you wish. The head will be large and fairly triangular compared to the norm, while the other proportions fall well within standard deviation for a human. Give the mantoid a warrior's broad shoulders.

2 Start to flesh out the line work of the body, using your guide. The hands taper to two claw-like fingers and a sharp thumb, while the feet are toeless triangles. The head is plectrum-shaped, with a thick neck to support it. Begin to clothe the mantoid in the protective garment he wears around the body, creating a bottom and a top garment.

3 Start with the head, adding in large, light-absorbing eyes. Note how the eyes reflect the shape of the head. Add two pinpricks for nostrils and a straight line for a mouth. The antennae are thin loops, like golf clubs, protruding from the top of the head. Segment the limbs at every joint, as shown. Complete with knee pads and boots.

4 Add shading to the eyes, ink and erase the pencil lines and proceed to colour. Light flesh tones contrast well against cool blues, with purple eyes as an accent.

> **Tip:** When creating a species, start with a 'benchmark' character that you can exaggerate and mutate to make individualized aliens.

Extended family

We know that ants are ruled by a queen, which is much larger than any other member of the species. Would you have a king or queen for this race, and would they be larger and very different from the rest? What kind of social structure would the mantoids possess? Worker mantoids, for example, could be adapted primarily for labour. You could assign a special role to the flying mants, making them the planet's police force. From here, it's a fairly straightforward process to develop ideas for the buildings and vehicles of your mantoid world, keeping the man/ant theme throughout.

Snapshot of a society ▶
You may find it helpful to create an image showcasing many different elements of your alien society in operation, trying to capture the 'essence' of what makes them tick. This picture shows a cross-section of mantoids engaged in the frantic act of hive construction, under the watchful and commanding eye of the queen.

Mecha giant robots

One of the most popular strands of science-fiction manga is that featuring mecha (short for mechanoid). Mecha are giant robots, at least one to two storeys tall (sometimes as large as several city blocks) and capable of insane amounts of damage. The difference between mecha and true robots is that mecha tend to be piloted by a human operative – often one specially chosen, born or bred for the purpose. Mecha proved very popular when they appeared in anime series such as *Gundam* in the late 1970s and early 80s. Mecha are often portrayed as Earth's – and humanity's – last, best hope against a similarly titanic alien menace: so why not pit your mecha designs against city-sized monsters and aliens?

Designing a robot

Using the human form as a basis is a good way to start dabbling with robot design, particularly if you haven't drawn any before. It also conforms neatly to the idea of a robot with a human pilot – when the pilot moves their arm or leg, the mecha duplicates their action on a far grander scale. Start with a basic human shape, but make variations in the outline, incorporating armoured segments and visible joints at every opportunity. If you've managed to design a few different human characters, it is only a few short steps from here into the mechanical world.

Rapid-fire machine ▶
Test your imagination. With each deadly weapon the size of two stretch-limousines, how will your mecha be resupplied in combat?

Combat weaponry ▲
Many human pilots create custom mecha that forego the flexibility of humaniform hands for the convenience of mounted weaponry, such as this hand-cannon and the shoulder rockets.

◀ **Command unit**
Even mecha built around the same chassis have the opportunity to be customized by their pilots. See if you can create a whole battalion from the same basic design, changing only the colours and head detailing.

Transforming jet ▶
Many mecha also incorporate a secondary, vehicular attack mode. This blue 'bot transforms into a 31st-century fighter jet.

Developing your mecha character

To make your mecha stand out, experiment with ways of
arranging its features in order to make them unique.
You don't have to obey any previous norms of mecha design.

Head ▶

Multiple lights or lenses, or a slit around the head that lights
up, often represent visual senses. A single eye could also flash
when the mecha 'speaks', transmitting the commands of its
pilot. As mecha generally magnify their pilot's body language
a hundredfold, an expressionless face may be the only
opportunity to maintain some reserve.

Shoulder-
mounted
sensors
transmit a
3-D view of
the battlefield
to the
cockpit.

This golden
faceplate
reflects light –
and lasers – to
protect the pilot.

This mecha's
digits can
retract in
favour of
twin pulse
cannons.

Sturdy feet keep
the weight of the
mecha anchored,
and house
projectiles and
flight capabilities.

Arms ▲

The arms need to look convincing, although they don't
necessarily have to be physically possible. For interesting
shape ideas, look to a mechanic's toolbox. You could choose
something like a hammer, upturn it, and use it as the upper
part of the arm that connects to the shoulder, with the head
of the hammer acting as the elbow. For the forearm, construct
a cylinder, add a few bumps for implied muscle, and rather
than end with a hand, choose a weapon, such as a miniature
cannon or a chainsaw blade.

◀ Legs

Instead of a cylinder, why
not choose a square-edged
shape for the thigh?
For the knee, draw a small,
turned-in block. Beneath
that, draw a giant foot-
shaped block that bends
off the knee by being
attached to either side of
it. Add enormous shin pads
that extend to the floor,
housing the heel but
leaving the foot/toe area
sticking out at the front.

Tip: It can be difficult to suggest the scale of humanoid robots.
When drawing them, be sure to surround them with visual clues,
whether in the shape of skyscrapers for them to tower over, standard
vehicles to crush, or human pilots climbing on board. Give the
reader's eye something to estimate height with.

Sidekicks and friends

You'll have noticed that it is extremely rare for a manga hero to walk around unaccompanied. In manga, the protagonists always have at least one or two companions who follow them on their journey. These are the supporting cast, the sidekicks, who come in many forms. They're not always people – a friend might be a creature, such as a pet or even an alien. This section, however, provides examples of some human sidekicks, who may help your lead in their quest.

The importance of a sidekick

When you create a sidekick, you add a further dimension to your story. Giving your protagonist a constant companion helps show the depths of his or her personality and, most importantly, gives them someone to have a dialogue with and explain the story to. Use yourself as an example and think about how your interaction with your friends, parents, teachers and bosses defines you as a person, in relation to others. Sidekicks are often a double-edged sword. Some are incredibly helpful, and may be more skilful than the lead character. Others, despite a wealth of technical skills or fighting prowess, are a constant hindrance to the main character. You could have a sidekick who is the lead character's best friend and always shows an unparalleled level of support. It could be that the this companion is over-confident and arrogant, leaping in, fists whirling whenever the lead character pleads for diplomacy or stealth. This would leave the protagonist frustrated at having to keep his companion's pugnacious nature under control.

Practice exercise: Genius

This sidekick is petite and slender, but makes up for what she lacks in muscles with the depth and breadth of her knowledge base. Fluent in dozens of languages, with a photographic memory, she's an irreplaceable asset to the main character.

Materials
- *soft lead pencil*
- *pen and ink*
- *colouring method of your choice*

1 Rough out the proportions of a standard female in her teens with a soft pencil, fleshing out your simple guidelines into a sketchy pose. To emphasize her IQ or her photographic memory, this genius points to her temple. She is examining some important documents clasped in her other hand and holds some papers under her arm. Keep the outline of your character minimal and the body slim. Sketch in some long hair, tied up at the back, with a ragged fringe (bangs) falling around to frame her face.

Tip: Glasses on a brainy character may be stereotypical, but in manga, common denominators are a way to establish characters quickly. You may decide to turn a stereotype on its head during the course of a story, subverting the expectations of your audience.

2 Give your character more definition with your pencil lines. Give the character narrowed, concentrating eyes and glasses over the top. Aim for a scientific-casual look with a lab coat, as if a PhD student has gone into the lab on her day off. Note the subtle sixth digit, giving her the appearance of being slightly unusual.

3 When you're satisfied with your pencil lines, ink them and erase the guidelines, and proceed to colour. Use a strong hair colour to direct attention to the character's head (and mammoth brain), and use colourful accents on the trousers and T-shirt to complement the stark white of the lab coat.

Practice exercise: Arrogant fighter

This guy is always in the mood for a fight, and while his physical presence may help the protagonist intimidate his opponents when they face enemies, thinking is not one of his special skills. He benefits from being around the cleverer lead, who does his best to keep him on a (metaphorical) leash.

Materials
• *soft lead pencil*
• *pen and ink*
• *colouring method of your choice*

1 Start with a rough set of guidelines, using a soft lead pencil. Unlike our protagonist, who might be around three heads wide from shoulder to shoulder, this character is around four to five heads wide and about six heads tall. Keep the head small, not much bigger than a normal head, to emphasize this character's limbs.

2 When defining the body, keep the neck wide to suit his muscular build. Arms and legs need to be broader than in a standard adult male, so that his physique emphasizes his strength. Define the main muscle groups to a greater degree than you usually would, particularly in the biceps, chest muscles and calves.

3 When detailing his face, give more definition to the nose and mouth. Keep his hair short with small spikes. Draw a tight, sleeveless T-shirt, keeping the arms exposed. Baggy shorts will give him freedom to kick. Add a heavy belt over the top. To show his past as a fighter, add a colourful tattoo around one arm.

4 When you're satisfied with your pencil lines, ink them and erase the guidelines, and proceed to colour. On this figure note that the skin is deeply tanned and his clothes plain, making the tattoo stand out in sharp relief.

Tip: It helps to get acquainted with your characters. Practise their proportions, and the most relevant poses likely to be used in a manga story. Keep a lasting record of all the characters you create to help maintain continuity and make sure that figures are not drawn incorrectly as your work progresses.

Elderly characters

Inevitably, since manga is a product of youth culture, elderly characters are not as prominent as their younger counterparts. When it comes to older sidekicks, manga tends to deal in two stock characters. The less common is the elderly martial arts sensei, who maintains an impressive physique even after several generations of fighting and teaching classes of young and boisterous students. The other is a mischievous character, often possessing special abilities. An elderly trickster will both lend the story some comic relief (inverting the 'respect your elders' paradigm) while, at the same time, constantly throwing complications into the path of the lead character as they try to get them out of trouble.

Practice exercise: Martial arts expert

This is a large character, almost imposing, but still in proportion, unlike the 'arrogant fighter' of the previous exercise. His strength and experience should be half-implied from his build, and half from the way he carries himself. Any up-and-coming student wouldn't dream of getting cocky. The martial arts expert is at his peak of fitness and keeps his moves disciplined, but his uniform has suffered over the years – think about whether you want to stick in rips and tears, or frayed edges. From a story perspective, consider why he'd want to carry on wearing this old uniform. Perhaps he wore it when he finally beat his own master in single combat.

Materials
- *soft lead pencil*
- *pen and ink*
- *colouring method of your choice*

1 Make the frame broad in the shoulders, and wider than the waist. This character's pose is inspired by many styles – this could be the beginning of a Mantis or Drunken Master move.

2 Dress your character, paying attention to the way the loose trousers and thick coat hang over his frame. The hair is close-cropped and the beard and moustache relatively long and thick around the lower part of his face.

3 Give definition to the face, adding wrinkles where appropriate. Make the eyes and eyebrows fairly angular, to convey his serious demeanour. Detail the frayed uniform and crease lines.

4 Move to colour, using classical earthen tones to suggest a grounded nature. Add shadows and highlights to give a 3-D effect.

Practice exercise: Crafty old wizard

This is an example of one of the more comical old characters, reminiscent of a chibi-style character, particularly as he's only going to be three heads high. His head will look quite large for his shoulders. If you decide to use a similar character in one of your stories, he could get his robes caught continually in doorways or be trodden underfoot to humorous effect.

Materials
* *blue pencil*
* *soft lead pencil*
* *pen and ink*
* *colouring method of your choice*

1 For the frame, make the shoulders and hips narrow. Keep the outline of his body thin but draw fully developed, rather than chibi-style, fingers. He will hold a long thin staff or broomstick that's over twice his height, so sketch a line into one clasped hand.

Tip: Remember, it's not only your hero who will be changed by the outcome of your narrative – his or her travelling companions may also undergo a metamorphosis, changing from good to bad, dying, changing forms or betraying the lead character and then sacrificing themselves to save them: all are possibilities along the way.

2 Sketch in large eyes, with an equally large grin and lines around the mouth. Draw pronounced cheekbones (when we age, features like the cheeks sink into the face, and the skin thins, so the bone structure of the skull becomes more obvious). Make a small, downward-pointing nose. Outline thick eyebrows and make the ears larger than normal, to divert attention to the head. Cover the wizard's receding hairline under an enormous pointed hat.

3 Finalize the features to give the face an impish expression and dress your character in a long robe that looks over-large, particularly at the sleeves. A high-collared cape flows out behind him. Draw a thin sash round his waist to draw his robes together, and add a small, hanging potions flask. Add texture lines to the broom and crease lines to the garments.

4 When you are happy with the final pencil drawing, ink over the lines and add colour. Choose hues and effects to enhance your character's traits, such as the glow added to this cackling wizard's unassuming broomstick. Add a familiar, such as this small pet frog, who will follow him everywhere.

Villains

Now you can move on to the bad guys. And let's face it, designing the villains is as much fun as designing your protagonist. This is your chance to create characters who will stop at nothing to defeat your protagonist. Often, a villain will have another motive as well, such as world domination, or a raging desire to destroy an entire city. Or your villain may be more subtle: a character who merely mirrors the protagonist, with similar abilities, like a rival in a sport which both characters play. Of course, the rival/villain resorts to cheating, while the protagonist always plays by the book.

Planning villains

When planning your villains, start with the main antagonist. Decide how you want them to look, and also the reasons why he or she and your main character are at odds. If you have a well-motivated, powerful antagonist, your protagonist's journey to his or her final confrontation will be tough and satisfying. It's crucial that your story of the protagonist's trials and tribulations is convincing. To this end, you should create a series of villains, escalating in toughness and evil, all guided by the near-omniscient hand of the master manipulator. Many shonen manga function like video games, with the protagonist defeating a series of 'bosses' in order to 'level up'. Ensure each 'boss' is engrossing and unique in order to maintain interest.

> **Tip:** Ensure the villain has all the latest equipment, gadgets and outfits at their disposal, putting them on a pedestal that the lowly protagonist can topple them from. Arrange for the hero and villain to meet, so you can highlight the extent of the differences between them.

Alien princess ▶
With thousands of ships at her disposal, this beautiful yet evil Martian princess is bent on domination of planet Earth. She has conquered a hundred worlds, and keeps all neighbouring planets under the yoke of her tyranny. But Earth will not bow, and she is constantly frustrated by its scuppering of her plans.

Vampire count ▲
This character has the feel of a classic manga villain. He is well dressed, powerful and good-looking. However, his glossy exterior hides less-reputable traits. Imagine him sitting high in his castle, holding the nearby town in his vice-like grip of terror. The moon is full, and the lord has sent his minions out for a fresh young bride to sate his bloodlust. Many strange creatures are at this villain's command, primed to stop any would-be hero from entering his domain.

◀ **High-school rival**
Your protagonist seems somewhat average in comparison to this guy, who is a youthful, charismatic all-rounder. However, he hates to lose, and his arrogance is often his undoing. Then again, with so many people thinking that he's the greatest, he rarely fails. It will take a particularly brave student to challenge him at what he does best, especially when others have been completely humiliated as a result of their failure.

Villain characteristics

As a general rule, keep your villains' features and clothing dark and dramatic. A protagonist dressed in lighter colours will provide contrast. Villains in manga are typically tall, and physically more impressive than the protagonist. Keep their eyes and eyebrows angular, so that they always look threatening. At the beginning of your story, your protagonist shouldn't have a hope of defeating your villain.

The idea is that he or she has to learn and train along the way. To make things more interesting, you might want to make your villain short on patience, so that anyone who dares to interfere with his plans will quickly fall victim to his temper – this can also include their various underlings.

Just as the hero or heroine has sidekicks, a villain always has aides: trusted henchmen, monsters of untold strength or manipulative strategists to advise them on their evil plans. But for every villain, there must be a flaw, a weakness, which will eventually be their downfall. Is it physical – an allergy to a potion or poison? Is it mental – a hubristic oversight to be exploited? With every villain you create, consider how your protagonist will discover their weaknesses and then make use of them to emerge victorious.

> **Tip:** Many great stories begin with the heroes or heroines having already lost – a land pillaged, a city destroyed or subjugated to a common enemy. Rallying your characters to unite against this defeat can be very satisfying.

◀ **Freshly made vampire**
The recently sired 'son' of the vampire count, his bloodlust and vigour are stronger than his father's. However, he still retains many of his human memories, which can cause conflict.

Werewolf enforcer ▶
Lycanthropic muscle-for-hire, this cut-off-wearing denizen of the night is a ferocious slayer of the innocent. But silver bullets can lay him down for good.

◀ **Tri-horn demon**
In return for asylum on Earth, this devilish rebel takes care of the count's enemies. However, if she displeases, she can be returned to Hell in the blink of an eye.

Supporting cast gallery

With a world of boundless possibilities ahead of you, it can often be difficult to find a place to start. With that in mind, this spread showcases some of the more esoteric combinations of attributes you can put together to create your supporting cast and their villainous antagonists. Remember to subvert expectations wherever you can – most, if not all, of these possibilities could work equally well for strange allies as for terrible adversaries, given a compelling backstory and reason to work alongside your heroic characters, rather than competing with them or devouring them.

Backup and adversaries

What makes a good character? An easily identifiable visual 'hook' always helps – many of the characters on this page are simple twists on the standard human physique, with alterations in colour and silhouette, and an inhuman feature such as horns or a tail.

The zombie ▶

This creation is a creepy twist on a 'normal' zombie character. The recognizable basics of human physiology are re-imagined as the 'living dead'. This shirtless zombie is emaciated and lacks coordination, his limbs stiffened and near-useless from rigor mortis. His clothing may be ripped or missing, and because of his emaciated state, will look several sizes too big. His face is a mess, with staring eyes and a gaping, dislocated jaw. For further fright, shade the eyes to shadows so they look almost hollow. The zombie communicates in moans; wind whistling over a grave.

Demonic faun ▲

Impish and mischievous, but not truly evil, this creature of the underworld enjoys nothing more than meddling in the plots and affairs of state.

◀ **Catgirl**

A hyper-evolved form of the common housecat, this sprightly, twin-tailed humanoid could be from the future, the result of a gene-blending experiment, or the magically uplifted form of a wizard's familiar. Perhaps she is indentured to her evil master, but longs to be free.

◀ Six-tailed fox
Neither good nor evil, but serving the capricious nature of the Universe, Six-Tailed Fox roams the highways of his fantasy dimension, directing and misdirecting travellers to new paths – and new fates. His magical tails allow him to fly.

Young Frankenstein's monster ▶
Stitched together from the corpses of a high school rock and roll band, this poor unfortunate wants nothing more than to rock out on the guitar, bass, drums and vocals, all at the same time. However, while he attempts to get his new life together, the scientist who resurrected him wants him to rob more corpses to create the ultimate girl band in one monstrous, immortal body.

Hydragon ▼
Cut one head off and two more will grow in its place, until eventually the hydragon will be so top-heavy that you can probably walk around it and steal whatever you like. In the meantime, though, it is a deadly, reptilian predator.

Mersorceress ▶
Born from a breed of humans who decided to follow the evolving dolphins back into the water, this mercreature practises an esoteric blend of water magic, one that requires the feeding of sacrificial victims to the Great Behemoth of the Deep.

Battle scene project

Every now and then it's great – and necessary – to draw good and evil into a massive conflict. It makes for a very satisfying payoff for your readers, and can be equally satisfying to draw. The main drawback is that it takes time, and can easily become confusing. Sometimes you can have two dozen characters on a single spread all involved in the fight, all performing a different action. As cool as it is to draw these entanglements, you should not make a habit of it. Manga – and stories in general – thrive on repeated waves of build-up and pay-off, so each great battle must be accompanied by a

similarly weighty section of plot development, a character-based 'fallow period' in between the waging of war. One way to keep track of your characters in these battles is to give each one a list of aims, goals and actions to undertake throughout, so that in each panel you know what all of your cast are doing.

▶ Good meets evil in a battle against a mecha warlord and his following.

Materials
- *soft lead pencil*
- *pen and ink*
- *colouring method of your choice*

1 List the characters involved in the fight, and their objectives within it; for example: 'Baron Von Struckmeer, a mecha-piloting local warlord wants to take

the head off the rebellious upstart Rainer Darksturm, so will ignore all lesser foes on the battlefield in order to engage him in hand-to-hand combat.'

2 Draw an overhead map of the battleground 'arena'. Wherever you are, making a map and tracing the positions of your combatants on it will allow you to keep a continuity of action from

any angle. When in doubt, create a couple of key 'landmarks' to anchor your action no matter which direction you view the fight from. Using your character objectives and overhead map, plot out your battle, panel by panel. Remember that your notes can be very brief: a note that 'X engages Y near to Z' is all you need. The map is there so that you can pick a spot on the map, choose a direction from which to view the action, and know at a glance what landmarks you will see from that direction. Try to rotate your 'camera' around the battlefield throughout your scene, alighting on the important struggles of each pair or group of main characters, even as you seek to capture the chaos of the larger, pitched battle raging around, in front and behind them.

CHARACTERS:
Rainer Darksturm
Baron Von Struckmeer

OBJECTIVE:
Kill or otherwise defeat the rebel Rainer Darksturm in hand-to-hand combat.

Will ignore all lesser threats.

3 When you have your plot of how the battle will flow, sketch out some thumbnails of your first spread. Keep the thumbnails small, and use stick figures or loose shapes to indicate where each of your characters will be placed. You may

want to start with a large overview panel of the entire battle, before zooming in to focus on individual fights – or you might want to start small, and zoom back to show the enormity of what is going on.

4 When you are happy that your thumbnails 'read' well, and that your battle, while chaotic, still flows from panel to panel, it's time to transfer your sketches to full-size pages and pencil, ink and render in colour your characters and backgrounds. Remember, too, that visuals and sound effects alone can often be enough to 'sell' a battle – the time for descriptive speech is long past, save for snarls and growls as long-time enemies lunge for each other's throats.

5 With larger-scale battles filled with complex elements and dozens of characters, you may find it easier to draw all of the panels individually, at a larger scale, before scanning them in, colouring them, and compositing them into your chosen layout. The beauty of creating thumbnails first is that it allows you to compose each panel as part of the final page so that each one flows correctly across the entire spread, regardless of whether you drew them all on the same scale or piece of paper.

Tip: If you are featuring characters in a number of different scales – humans and giants, for example, or humans and mecha – remember to show how each of these scales relate to one another, and how they interact within the fight. This can be as simple as showing two humans battling in the shadow of an enormous foot, or as complex as two people scaling the artificial mountain of a striding mecha in order to pull out its control cords.

Narrative and layout

Now that you have learned how to create characters and settings, weapons, props and vehicles, it's time to take what you have learned about manga to the next level, and see what it takes to assemble a story. From crafting your overall narrative to creating a finished page from concept to colours, this chapter will guide you through every step.

What's in a story?

Your story is the most important element of your manga. Artwork and dialogue, no matter how polished, are all created in service of your narrative. Manga is a medium of narrative told through sequential art – each panel building on the one that went before it, melding words and pictures to create a sequence that accurately communicates the intent of the writer and artist. The story must keep your reader engrossed throughout, leading gradually to a climactic ending. In this section, you'll learn the basic tools of page-to-page storytelling: using images in sequence, building suspense and releasing tension, framing images in panels, and arranging your panels to control pace and flow.

Narrative rhythm

Within every story, you need to convey meaning and sustain interest, but you must also reveal your story effectively, in a logical order. Arrange the events of your story so that your audience can follow the action easily, and try to make the drawings and dialogue flow together to create a good narrative rhythm. Such rhythms are controlled by your choice of shots: long, wide panels will slow the eye down, as will large sections of dialogue, while small, choppy, silent panels will prove exceedingly quick to read. A mixture of both – and every step in between – will allow you to pace each scene as appropriate to its content. Different genres may have different rhythms: a shonen action manga will be relatively faster and choppier than a more contemplative shojo romance.

Preoccupation with surroundings punctuates the romantic moment

Shadowed panel builds suspense and mystery

White space creates expectation of action to follow

'Widescreen' panels create langorous pacing

Wide shot slows down the moment so we appreciate the scale of battle and the length of the sword swing

Close-ups make us focus on eyes and characters' interior lives

Shonen 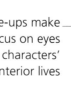▲
This page literally bursts with action, with its warrior protagonist extending out of the boundaries of every panel, her sword providing the focus that draws us down the page. Note the use of negative space to create mystery and expectation of the action to come.

Shojo ▶
This romantic story, on the other hand, provides plenty of opportunity to focus on what the characters are saying or thinking, as everything but their faces has dropped out of the frame. The wide panels replicate awkward or thoughtful pauses in conversation.

Narrative movement

The way the reader's eye moves across the page is called the narrative movement. Keeping control of this keeps readers interested. It's important to think in terms of character and camera movement – a dialogue scene of 'talking heads' that repeats the same heads for pages on end will kill momentum and reader sympathy dead. Keep your 'camera' moving around static cameras, or keep your characters moving even as they talk. It is crucial to keep this movement in order to maintain the energy of each scene. Change between close-ups, mid-shots and long shots depending on the tenor of the dialogue: focusing on the surroundings as a character's attention wanders; cutting to an extreme close-up when a character reveals shocking information.

Conversation on the move ▶
The two characters meet in a long-shot, before cutting to a close-up of the first character to speak.

Drama, action and tension

Your stories will need tension. If, for example, your story is designed to be split into instalments, you will need your audience to want to come back for more at the end of each chapter. In a murder mystery, for instance, the detectives will start with the body alone, but as the story progresses, they will collect evidence and clues to lead them to the perpetrator – with plenty of twists and turns along the way. It's up to you to reveal your clues and moments of shock and suspense at the optimum points in the story.

Storytelling doesn't depend solely on dialogue. In some instances, you may wish to let the action speak for itself.

◀ Kidnap, mugging or murder?
Tension builds because the reader is aware of the danger the girl faces from the first panel, while the girl is oblivious – until her attacker vaults from the shadows! What happens next? We can't help but turn the page.

Moving around the setting

Sequences tend to spread over more than one panel – whether they are fights or conversations. How do you create the flow of a sequence? Here we have two characters in conversation. One is asking for directions from the other. The first panel is a shot of the characters from the waist up, facing one another. The dialogue is: 'Do you know the way to the police station?' Instead of giving the answer as to where it is located in this shot, the reply is illustrated in the next panel, which also changes the angle, a 'camera move' to maintain interest. The conversation flows across the panels, the reader's eye is drawn from one panel to the next, and their interest is piqued, maintained and satisfied within the space of two frames. The second panel is a close-up of the character answering.

Practise keeping conversations interesting. Take a similar pair of characters and create an extended dialogue between them. Focus on how the listener and the speaker react to each other. Start with a view over the shoulders of the first speaker, perhaps, so that we can't see the expression on their face, only how the listener is reacting, then swap the view in the second panel. Practise mixing long shots, mid-shots and close-ups.

Getting directions ▼
How would you continue this exchange? Would you add dialogue, or segue into the young character's journey to the police station?

Change of location

This device is often used to change scenes and locations in a more fluid and natural manner than with a narrative caption (e.g. 'Four Hours Later...', 'In a Warehouse Downtown...'). The first panel of the new scene shows either an exterior shot of a building with a speech balloon directed towards it, or the exterior of a room, with a speech balloon similarly placed.

In the example to the right, a female investigator is eavesdropping at a locked office door. The following panel cuts to a view of the person who is speaking, and the new scene proceeds from there.

Be careful to only shift back to an exterior view when beginning a new sequence, or when adding emphasis that require a long shot of the characters' location, as hopping back and forth between interiors and exteriors will only confuse your reader.

◄ Eavesdropping
The private investigator in question has arrived at the new location just in time to hear the details (and remarkably low price) arranged for her own demise.

Behind the door ▶
When the telephone is replaced in its cradle, she makes her move, drawing her handgun and bursting into the office!

Length of dialogue

Dialogue delivers crucial details concerning the characters and their motives, but too much slows the pace and ruins the timing you're trying to establish. You match your dialogue to the artwork and the narrative rhythm. In fast-paced sequences especially, don't let dialogue dictate the speed. If you have a sequence showing a character running towards a building – they're late for school, say, as shown here – don't *state* the reasons why they're late; they don't have time. Keep the dialogue succinct to emphasize their speed – and breathlessness. Explanations can come later.

Sense of urgency ▲
As the two students bolt out of their apartment block, the emphasis in the dialogue is on reinforcing the main reason why they're running – they're late – without going into any further detail.

Busted! ▲
Now the story shifts down gears, as the students get a chance to explain themselves.

No need for dialogue

Sometimes you don't need dialogue at all, as the action itself will reveal the drama. Your characters shouldn't describe through dialogue what is shown – it's repetitive, slows the pace, and implies your audience needs assistance. In this example, the destruction of one jet fighter by another is clearly depicted without the need for commentary.

Deadly dogfight ▶
The black jet fighter swoops in (1); achieves a target lock on the blue jet (2); fires a homing missile (3) that targets blue's engines (4); the missile detonates (5), and the blue jet plummets out of the sky on fire (6). Note the use (or lack) of borders on the panels, and the use of spot sky blue in the bottom two panels.

Tip: When pacing scenes, choose moments that actually drive your story along – don't string out brushing teeth or making coffee over six pages in an effort to 'build tension', unless your story involves possessed toothpaste or a poisoned espresso.

Composing the panel contents

Knowing what to place within a panel, and how to build and release narrative tension, is extremely important in manga. As with composing a frame of film, the contents of a panel must direct the reader's eye to what is most important about this snapshot of the scene. Unlike film, manga panels can disregard extraneous background information – there's usually no need to draw anything that isn't essential to the ongoing story, and this can often involve backgrounds dropping out at moments of high tension, or detailed facial work on background characters being kept to a minimum. Each panel should show the reader exactly what they need to know, and work as part of a sequence. In quick-paced manga, the storyteller often only has a few panels to build tension – especially when working to a weekly schedule.

Provide a focus

Each panel must have a focus, and the art should guide the audience to that centre. Keep the contents of each panel varied, to add interest. Don't draw your characters from the same angles all the time, or with the same facial expressions. You need to vary the appearance and perspectives of the characters to reflect their mood, situation, or what they are saying.

A lesson in contrasts ▶
The strips shown here communicate the same information in very different ways. The first repeats the same art, in the same way as comic strips found in many newspapers, while the second mixes angles, expressions and colour backgrounds to far more vibrant effect.

The strips begin the same way, with a two-shot of the talking characters.

The first strip re-uses the first panel all the way through, with only minor variations, relying on the dialogue to drive the story.

The mixture of panel widths and colours in the second strip creates art bursting with energy.

Abstract backgrounds illustrate character's emotions.

Composition

It is very important that your audience is shown exactly what they need to see. For example, if you are showing a company boss giving a speech to a boardroom full of directors or employees, the boss should be the focus of the majority of your panels, because he is the central speaker. By all means start with a long shot to establish the boss's location and placement with regards to the rest of his employees, but assist the flow of the story and the focal point of the scene by locking your 'camera' on to the speaker. If the boss singles out a particular employee in his speech, by all means insert a panel to show that employee's reaction, but then cut back to the boss as he continues his diatribe. If he opens the meeting up to questions, you could create a new panel establishing how the employees feel, before they respond.

Long shot establishes scale of boardroom and relation of characters to one another.

Perspective directs eye to far end of table, and the boss sitting there.

Backgrounds drop out, save for chair and downlight, to emphasize the boss character.

Shadowy boardroom ▲
Although the body language of the board is tense, it's clear that there is only one chairman in this room – and he has a lot of angry things to say.

Laying out the page

The best way to plan out a sequence is to sketch out the panels in relation to the whole page. Remember that manga compositions rely on whole pages, and sequences, for their effect, and designing and illustrating panels in isolation will never give you the best results.

Symmetrical layout and panels ▶

Pages that are symmetrically composed like this have no centre of attention, nothing to draw the eye to any significant part of the page. The eye flits from left to right, left to right, which can make for dull reading. Symmetrical layouts are mostly used for conversations, in which characters are imparting information to one another. If you use a grid like this throughout your story, it has the benefit of becoming 'invisible', like a picture frame or a TV screen through which the action is viewed. This is also the format for Japanese four-panel gag strips, which, unlike those in the West, are arranged vertically and reprinted two to a page.

Asymmetrical layout ▶

For a more showy, graphical approach, you can create designed, asymmetrical pages, which use the size and shape of each panel to showcase their relative importance, control pacing and drive the reader's eye around the page. This is a style of composition that draws a lot more attention to itself, making the act of layout a part of the story itself and keeps the reader on a rollercoaster ride across the page. Using different angles and rotated, unconventional panels maintains drama and interest in what is happening on the page – sustain this across a sequence, and your audience will be hooked for the journey.

Tip: Panel size matters. The larger the panel, the more emphasis you place on it. Smaller panels increase pace. The smaller the panel, the less detail you can render, and the faster the reader takes it in and moves on.

Using the same size panel for every image creates a conformity of importance across the strip, where every image carries equal weight.

The repetition of the same frame across the pages causes the reader to focus on its contents, rather than the method of delivery (the shape of the panel).

Irregularly shaped bubble for dramatic effect.

Large panel with plenty of emphasis.

Pace is slowed. Background dictates a thoughtful pose.

Unconventional panels give the cartoon a fresh feel and look.

Narrative dramatization in panels

The use of perspective in your panel frames will not only help the look of the page, but can also set the pace or increase the drama of your story. There are a wide, even infinite, variety of perspectives from which to view your art (close-up, medium view, wide-angle to name just a few) which you can use in your art. For the time being, use a selection of the examples shown here: they are all you need to tell a compelling story and create good-looking pages.

Common types of panels

Some panel shapes are termed 'neutral' and allow the art to dictate the pace of the story. Others speed up the pace, encouraging the reader's eye to race around the page.

Standard view ▲
This panel reveals a lot of information at a character level, demonstrating a character's visual identity, through their clothing and accessories, as well as their stance, motivation and expression. It also encompasses detail of the character's immediate environment, allowing a reader to keep track of them as they move through a location.

Wide-angle view ▲
Panels that provide a wide-angle view are often used to introduce new locations or cut to a new scene. They are often half a page high, but can be extended to single or double-page spreads to increase their impact. They can effectively establish a new story or add dramatic impact to an event. If you have two mythical warriors facing one another with their swords drawn, for instance, a wide-angle panel gives you space to set the scene, showing the characters in relation to their environment.

Medium view ▲
A waist-up shot allows the reader to focus on the character's expression while also including more visual cues about their clothing, weaponry and stance than a pure head shot.

Western comic panel ▲
Heavily influenced by the grammar of film, this type of panel shows the character mainly from the waist up, but may go down as far as the knees. It is used to emphasize a character's stance and emotional state. The legs aren't necessarily included, as they are the least expressive part of the body. Such panels also provide a detailed view of the character's environment.

Close-up view ▲
This dramatic view concentrates the reader's focus purely on the character's expression, tightly cropping the shot around the character's head. Shading or colour giving an impression of the character's emotional state may be used in the background, or it may be left blank, as in this example, to emphasize the facial features.

Plot shot ▲

Another type of close-up panel, this time focused on something that is intrinsic to the development of the story, with relevance to the narrative: here, a figure well disguised against the background lurks in the shadows.

Horizon ▲

A natural-looking panel shape that resembles the perception we have of our surroundings in real life. There is typically a character in the foreground, and the horizon of the story's environment in the background.

Bird's-eye view ▲

A dramatic device, looking down on a character. It can establish the character in their environment at the start of a story, or highlight a dangerous situation by making the character smaller in relation to the dangerous object or entity in the foreground, demonstrating a character's vulnerability and the struggle they face.

◀ **Tilt**

This panel conveys everything on a slant, offering an unbalanced view that adds tension and uncertainty. The background may consist simply of speed lines in a circular zoom formation, pointed at the character's head, which is a good way of freezing time for an instant to emphasize the character's tension or alarm.

Tatami view ▲

This view is derived from the Japanese tradition of sitting on tatami mats on the floor while eating. The horizontal view is used to show two characters, usually in a historical setting, having a discussion across a meal or in a hut. *Blade of the Immortal* and *Lone Wolf and Cub*, both set in feudal Japan, often use this view.

Mouse's-eye view ▲

The opposite of the bird's-eye view, this panel conveys a character's strength and superiority, making a character dominant within the panel. It can also make the reader feel threatened and insignificant by proxy.

Panel shapes and sizes

The panels are the individual pieces of artwork in the sequence of your story, and each is defined by the frame (or lack thereof) that surrounds it. Frames can be anything from a simple black line that divides each panel from one another (leaving the 'gutter' or white space between) to intricately rendered pieces of baroque architecture that, by calling attention to themselves, reveal as much about the setting and period of the story as their contents. See for yourself how altering the frame can change the intent and effect of your artwork by copying the same piece of action on to a single sheet of paper several times. Render some panel borders around the pictures using the examples shown here.

Main panel and frame types

Some panel shapes are only used for specific occasions, while others will crop up constantly throughout a story. You may develop your own shapes with time, but the six panel shapes illustrated here provide a good foundation.

Open panel ▲
This is a boundless panel that is used during a scene where the character is lost in thought or taking stock of their surroundings. The pace is definitely slowed by using this technique, and not putting a boundary around the art allows it to stop and take a breather. It is the comic-book equivalent of a dramatic pause in a film as it throws all of the focus on to the character.

YOU'RE SLIPPING, SENSEI. TIME WAS THE SCENT OF HAZELNUTS IN YOUR SAKI WOULD HAVE HAD YOU SCREAMING 'POISON'. THE DOJO IS MINE NOW.

Standard frame ▲
Square or rectangular, and drawn in a regular fashion, the standard frame's main use is to call as little attention to itself as possible, merely dividing two pieces of action from one another.

Tip: Any shape can be used to create a panel, but be warned that a story full of star shapes, dodecahedrons and similar shapes may drive away more readers than it impresses. Panels are there to contain your artwork, not overshadow it.

Parallelogram frame ▶
Essentially a standard frame with the left and right 'walls' tilted to one side, this panel is used to add pace and verve to action sequences. Its shape psychologically influences the reader to flip through the pages at a faster pace. The panel should slant in the direction the audience is reading.

◄ Cloud panel

The cloud panel has a specific use in manga, usually indicating a sequence of daydreams, nightmares, flashbacks or similar. The softer, rippled edges of these panels are the standard method of establishing that reality has taken a back seat, and the character's imagination and subconscious have been thrown to the fore.

Trapezium pairs ▶

Used for fast, focused scenes, these frames normally involve extreme close-ups on the point of action. They are generally drawn as a pair within the space of a single standard panel. Because they are small and angular, they help propel the action forward. In this example of a sword fight, one panel shows a rapid parry between the swords, the second shows the protagonists circling for another swing. Both focus purely on the motion of the blades. The second example shows the two swordsmen, each reacting to the way the fight is going. Placing both trapezium pairs on the same page fulfils the same function as rapid cuts between cinematic close-ups in a chaotic action sequence.

Tip: These panels work best for simultaneous moments: the panels show a moment of time literally sliced in half and apportioned to each of two points-of-view.

◄ Panel with 'jaggies' (jagged edge)

The jagged edges of this panel help convey a dangerous situation, or illustrate a violent act as it is committed by a character. These tend to be used singularly, with never more than one per page, or the rhythm of the piece would be jeopardized. Think of this as the exclamation mark of sequential framing, and use it sparingly. The reader only needs to be told once that the coming sequence is rife with danger. Then they want to see the action you've just brought to their attention.

Laying out an entire page

To lay out a page, you use a variety of panels of differing shapes, each appropriate to their content and importance, to present one sequence out of your larger story. Creating a sequential narrative is not something to undertake in a haphazard fashion. Each panel must flow into the next, with links according to shape, content and dialogue, so that the sequence follows a logical progression in the eye and mind of the reader. When laying out a page, consider yourself a one-person film unit. Your actions alone decide how fast or slow the story moves, based on the panels' size, content, shape and frame (or lack of). Why not try reworking an existing page of your favourite manga, deliberately altering the pacing? Bear in mind that, in the West, we read from left to right – this will affect how you design your page.

Panel sequence

Each panel is a point in time in your story. The page is a collection of these points, each following on from the previous panel, while also simultaneously existing as a coherent whole. It's the artist's job to make the page work in unison, carrying the reader through the story in a natural and fluent manner. When laying out a page, you need to make sure your panels follow each other in a way that the reader understands. Arranging the panels obscurely as an artistic flourish will only serve to hamper your storytelling, as readers will spend more time working out what comes next than focusing on the panel they are reading. Take a look at the examples. One is simple, running left to right in a zigzag down the page, the other is based on a single, dominant image.

Note how the speech balloons also guide the eye down the page from top left to bottom right.

Predominance of background in first panel subtly draws attention to the windows – and what is outside them.

Cutting off the character's eyes focuses us on his mouth – and his dialogue.

Tip: Traditional manga is read from right to left. Because of the increasing popularity of 'real' manga (and the cost of 'flopping' the artwork) many books are now being reprinted in their original direction. Try laying out pages from right to left as well as left to right.

Reversed direction of glare on glass is subtle continuity clue tying in to the first panel.

Highlighted character guides the reader's attention across the panel towards the speaker under surveillance.

Make it interesting ▶
Note the extreme differences in shading between the deep blacks of the character in the bushes and the brightly lit, almost sterile quality of the room it is observing.

The page as a whole presents a switch in viewpoint, from the children in the room to the skulker in the bushes.

Tip: You don't have to use panels that are a regular shape throughout an entire page – the reader's interest may flag. Instead, think about how you can vary your shapes to increase the interest and appeal of your layout.

Call-outs on a splash page ▶
This design is useful for a slower, dialogue-based sequence, or a shocking moment that needs time to sink in. The panels with extreme close-ups of the characters' faces could almost be occuring at the same time as the large image, which forms the backdrop and sets the timing for the whole page.

One of the strengths of manga over film is that it allows you to present and view both the close-up and the long shot at the same time.

These narrative captions offer us the girl's thoughts during the dominant, backlit panel.

Again, note how much good balloon placement has to do with controlling the direction of flow on a page.

The reader is invited to linger over these full figures – like the blonde-haired character, the reader is caught like a rabbit in the headlights.

Tip: Only move on to double-page spreads when you are confident you can control the flow of story across two linked pages. Bear in mind that people are used to reading a single page at a time, and may read them out of sequence.

Web comic panel layout

Web comics follow slightly different rules. While it's true that many are laid out in the same manner as traditional printed comics with a number of panels on each page, in practice you can flout the rules of page and panel layout. In an electronic format, you are not restricted by a page count, or by the number of panels you can fit on the page.

If you work electronically, you could just as easily lay out a single panel at a time, creating what is essentially an electronic storyboard, whereby the importance of keeping your audience no longer depends upon planning the page along with everything else, but instead concentrates far more on each panel being well composed by the artist. The need for each panel to communicate its action well becomes paramount, because the reader will move from one to the next a lot faster than if they had an entire page of panels to get through. In fact, your narrative rhythm is driven purely by how much information you give the reader in each panel.

Traditional web comic layout ▲
This web comic uses a traditional manga page layout, allowing the viewer to scroll through the page from top to bottom (the page is sized so that it fits the width of the screen). Each new page can be reached through a link that 'turns' the virtual page. Surprises in the story can be hidden at the bottom of the page so that they aren't seen at the same instant the page loads.

Dialogue and speech balloons

Once your page layout is decided, you can add dialogue and captions. Character dialogue emphasizes and adds a secondary (potentially antagonistic) layer to the actions depicted. It also demonstrates your characters' verbalized motivation and carries the majority of their interactions with one another. Dialogue is housed within speech balloons, or speech bubbles as they're sometimes called. Thought balloons are the equivalent for the unspoken, though fashions sometimes dictate that thoughts are written in caption boxes. Remember to leave space for your balloons when drawing your panels or you will end up obscuring your artwork when it comes to adding them later. Most readers tend to read the balloons first and focus on the artwork second, so use your balloons to guide your reader's eyes.

Placing balloons

Placing balloons is as much a science as an art, but bear in mind that a balloon larger than a third of the panel space available is excessive, and that balloons, like panels, are read from top left to bottom right, and must be placed accordingly if more than one character is talking. Nowadays, most speech balloons are placed by computer, but there are still artists who prefer the traditional method of using templates to draw balloons on to the page. If this includes you, pencil in your balloon and text first, and ink afterwards.

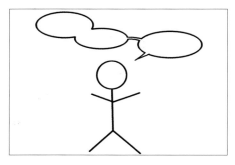

Balloon placement in panel ▲
The above example shows how you can replicate pauses in dialogue within a single panel. Short pauses can be shown by 'budding' balloons off of other balloons, while longer pauses require a complete break – perhaps joined by a thin 'tail' between two balloons.

Balloon flow ▶
This example shows how dialogue has been placed to guide the eye across and down the page, in a manner that also takes pains not to cover up any important areas of the artwork.

Balloon shapes

Although the dialogue within a balloon will help reveal a character's emotional state, the shape of the balloon itself can further emphasize it.

The four most common shapes ▲
Dialogue delivered in a normal way (without extreme emphasis) is contained in the standard, rounded-edged, rectangular or ovular shapes. All finish in a small point, or 'tail' that indicates who is speaking. Japanese bubbles are tall not wide, as the dialogue is written in vertical columns.

Captions describing a place or a scene ▲
Although rare in manga, captions describing a place, or setting a scene, are sometimes included. Essentially, this is the neutral voice of a narrator, allowing you to cut to a different point in time, or to move between characters in different locations, with phrases such as 'meanwhile, across town' or 'later that day'. Captions are most commonly delivered in a rectangle in an establishing panel.

Sound effects ▲
Mainly shown without a speech balloon, these represent sounds made by the characters, objects, accessories, and pieces of scenery. Gunshots, someone knocking on a door, a door creaking and the sound of footsteps on the floor are some common examples.

Inner feelings and thoughts ▲
Use cloud balloons for thoughts. Instead of a tail, a series of smaller clouds or bubbles lead to the balloon. In humorous stories, a simple illustration to show the character's thoughts can be used instead, as in this example.

Dotted-line balloons ▲
Used to convey a quiet voice or a whisper, these balloons are not used much in manga. A more common method is to use a standard bubble with the text written smaller than it would be for a normal speaking voice.

Jagged-edge balloons ▲
These balloons are used to convey a character's extreme emotion or a loud 'outside' voice, such as a character who is screaming in pain, shouting with anger and aggression, or yelling a warning to someone.

Panel shapes gallery

This spread contains a veritable cornucopia of further examples of panel shapes, page layouts and balloon placements. Take note of how the colour of your gutters influences the mood of the page – try adding in blues, reds and greens and seeing what effect they cast over your stories. Examine, too, how the use of different colours – and different fonts – in your speech balloons can imply different voices, strange languages and unfamiliar tongues.

More panels, page layouts and speech bubbles

The purpose of each panel is to show the reader the elements, characters and situations that will take him or her through the story keeping their interest throughout. It is the managa-ka who selects the most appropriate panel for each scene to show the reader the essential elements to understand the plot. Each panel is part of thinking about a whole page.

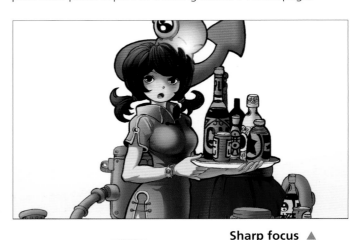

Sharp focus ▲
The background of this panel drops out to focus on the girl and the paraphernalia surrounding her.

Oval-shaped panel ▲
The shape focuses the eye on the shining wand, and carries through the soft and cute shape of the characters.

Cinematic horror ▲
The 'widescreen' panels and black borders create a cinematic feel and give plenty of scope for background detail.

◄ **Cloud dreams**
Hooked up to a dream-influencing terminal, this character's lucid dreams take her into various fantastic scenarios – with the cloud borders delineating the boundaries of the real and dreamed.

Explosive panel ▲
The explosive shape of the panel adds visual interest to an activity that is, in reality, rather dull. Hacking firewalls sounds a lot more exciting in theory than in practice.

Jagged balloon ▲
A character slips and begins to curse –
the perfect opportunity for a jagged
balloon and a loud exclamation.

New balloon colouring ▼
This illustration, featuring non-
standard balloon colouring, has a
creative, but highly readable, layout.

Superimposed panels ▲
Inset panels are close-ups superimposed
over wider shots. This is a 'teaser' panel,
not showing the bath straight away.

Thought-speech bubble ▲
Although the boy would never complain
out loud, he can say whatever he wants
in the privacy of his own head.

Colour border ▲
When it gets too much for the sorcerer,
his assistant gets a chance to shine in this
panel bordered only by colour.

Sketching thumbnails

Most manga creators, even those both writing and drawing their story, prefer to write a script as a guide before starting to illustrate their tale. Scripts contain brief descriptions of the characters and action in each panel, along with any dialogue and captions. The first step in transferring your script to the page as illustrations is to 'thumbnail' your script as a series of small sketches, showing the position of characters, the angles you have selected to best show the action, and the size of each panel in relation to the others. This way, you can spot any compositional problems before you start drawing for real.

Why thumbnail?

Once you have completed your script, you need to plan the look of your pages, making some panels more dominant than others, choosing your close-ups and long shots and spotting any areas where an obtuse passage in the script may need to be made more clear through an additional panel or some expositionary dialogue. Thumbnails are named for their relative size – while not literally the size of a thumb, you should be able to sketch an entire page on half a sheet of A4, or half that again. The small size makes you focus on what is truly important in each panel, and to view each panel as an element of the whole page. You may find it useful to spot areas of light and shade at this scale as well, colouring areas of shadow in a way that makes the page easier, rather than harder, to read.

Thumbnailing may seem like an extra stage, and it's natural to want to get stuck into putting your art on to the page as soon as possible, but the more problems you solve during thumbnailing, the less chopping and changing you'll have to do later. It's also worth thinking about pacing – would a page work better if the final panel was moved to the next page and given more space, for instance? Does a reveal need a full page all of its own? Are some sections moving sluggishly, others cramming too much in?

Keeping it simple ▲
Thumbnails are illustrations stripped to the absolute basics. Choose only the data that allows you to see whether a panel's composition is working, and enough to remind you of what you need to draw. Leave everything else out, keeping anatomy to stick-men or rough sketches, if you prefer (adding an eyeline to show where a character is looking can often be a useful addition), and backgrounds to symbolic shapes and squiggles.

Tip: Thumbnails are the first stage in drawing a finished page – not the point at which you begin to design your characters and costumes. However, they can also be useful for a writer/artist in a hurry: rather than spending time in a script describing characters, locations and actions with which they are familiar, they can leapfrog straight to the thumbnail script stage, playing around with layouts and dialogue on the same page.

Planning the details

The thumbnail stage is the point at which to make sure the art you have planned for is going to fit, particularly considering speech balloons. Focus your problem-solving attention on text-heavy panels: there is no point trying to fit in lots of detail if it will be covered up. Make sure the panels you have laid out give you sufficient space for the characters you want to appear, any background that is necessary to suggest location, and all of the required dialogue. This is also an excellent opportunity to edit your script. Writing your dialogue and stage directions in isolation is one thing, but you may change your mind when you see the art laid out on the page. Take the time to trim balloons that are too long, or add in extra ones to help smooth any awkward panel transitions.

Balloon placement ▼

Thumbnails are also great opportunities to test ways of controlling the flow of the reader's eye across the page, as with the sketched balloons below.

Thumbnail practice

To practise thumbnails, here's a relatively simple exercise. Choose a favourite or familiar manga and draft a script based on five to ten pages, writing down the descriptions of the setting, character, action and dialogue in each panel. Now close the manga, and, using your script, create your own thumbnailed versions of the pages, choosing the size and shape of the panels and presenting the action as you see fit. When you have finished, compare your versions of the pages to the final result – how close are they? Which version do you prefer? You may find that the thumbnails are close, as you are familiar with the existing pages, or you may find you have improved on the layout and panel flow! If you have a friend or fellow artist who is also learning to create manga, why not transcribe a script each and then swap? That way, you'll be approaching the script completely fresh, and may be even more pleasantly surprised by the results.

Same script, different story ▲

The aim of thumbnails is to save you time later by allowing you to experiment at a much smaller scale. Focus on bold shapes and whole-page compositions: worrying about the details is for later.

Creating roughs

The roughs are the next stage in refining your manga strip, offering a halfway house between the near-abstract planning of the thumbnails and the ready-for-print detail of the pencilling and inking stages. Roughs are all about experimentation and artistic problem-solving, refining the stick-men and blobby backgrounds of your thumbnails on the same scale as your actual art. While some artists produce roughs on a separate sheet and then transfer the line work to a fresh sheet of paper using a lightbox, other artists produce their roughs and finished pencils on the same page, refining one into the other. For those working in digital colour, on pages that will be scanned, many artists use blue-line pencils for their rough stage, followed by HB pencils for their finished line work. Whether scanned in as pencils or inked and then scanned, the blue lines are not picked up by the scanner, producing cleaner reproductions with less messy erasing.

Roughing it

Unlike thumbnails, your roughs should be done to the scale of the finished art, and should contain a lot more detail. One way to start laying out roughs is to blow up your completed thumbnails to actual size and either transfer them to a fresh sheet on the lightbox or redraw them by eye, using the originals as reference. You will hopefully find that your redrawn versions are better than your originals in many ways.

Thumbnails are all about speed and generalized compositional problem-solving, in that most artists use very simple shorthands for their figures, from stick-people to circles with lines indicating the direction of view. Backgrounds are usually absent or consist of boxes and lines. Roughs, on the other hand, are about expanding these simple notes and directions into something approximating the finished page. You need to flesh out anatomy ensure that it's in proportion, and make sure that perspectives mesh with any items and characters they share panels with. Don't be afraid to redraw challenging aspects of your page until you are satisfied with them – roughs are about saving you time later on.

Tip: While each of these stages is designed to give you and your drawing ability more thinking and problem-solving time, you may find as you develop – and as the deadlines come knocking – that you begin to combine different stages to make the whole process quicker. Don't be ashamed about taking shortcuts to deliver timely art – it's what the manga industry is based on, after all – but be sure you aren't doing your talents a disservice at any stage.

Tightening the layout ▲
A confident artist would have no trouble inking a final page from these lines, at 1:1 scale, block in accurate proportions and indicate all areas of background. Take particular note of the lack of shading or line width differentiation, however.

Rough backgrounds

Roughs allow you to sketch out a more established view of the scenery in your story, working from the details included in your initial script. As well as working on the anatomy of your characters, you should fill out and block in the proportions of your backgrounds, using photo reference, collated sketches, or your own imagination. If working from reference, block in backgrounds in the rough stage, but try not to refer back to your reference when drawing your finished pencils, so keeping a looser and more imaginative line. The main thing to think about at the roughs stage is integration: do your characters convincingly exist within their environment? Does the background overwhelm the character work, or detract from an important emotional moment? If so, now is the time to scale back your detail, or drop a background from a panel altogether. If your roughs show too little background information, now is the time to scout for suitable reference or inspiration.

If you're drawing your roughs on a separate sheet of paper, you can always refer back to them if and when you get stuck. Treat them as a 'first draft'. If you've drawn them on the same sheet as your roughs, your artwork will evolve as you incorporate each new stage of detail into the drawing. The more confident you can be when you put your final lines on the page the less likely you'll be to need an eraser.

Complete composition ▲
This is another example of a rough page in which all of the basic character information is present. All that remains is to add a further stage of detail, shading, line weight and visual flair.

◄ **Figure-drawing roughs**
This image, with its intricate foreground detail and involved figurework, requires some thought in the rough composition before you start to draw the thousands of leaves. Here's the rough with the completed artwork.

Inking and finishing off the page

So you're finally ready to bring everything together. Now you can pencil your first page for real. You've designed your characters, your setting, and the story that brings it all together. You've laid out the pages and checked that each set of panels flows well and is easy to understand. You may have worked ahead and thumbnailed your entire story before you begin to draw the first page to a finished standard, so check

that your story builds to a satisfying conclusion. Give everything a final check before you set to work. Do your layouts work on each page? Have you illustrated what you need to show from your script, or have you been distracted by 'cool' but unimportant things to draw along the way (and have you shied away from aspects necessary but tricky to draw?). When you're ready, take a deep breath and dive in.

Finishing touches

Keep final pencil lines clean and tight so they are ready for inking.

Background ▶
Note the use of very sparse backgrounds, only showcasing elements absolutely essential to the storytelling, such as the door and the staircase.

Detail ▶
This is the stage to check whether everything is correct: lines, balloons and detail.

▼ **Inking** The finished pencils are inked for easier scanning, and because the lines will hold colour better.

◀ **Palette** The colour palette is very limited: a rich range of reds and browns, save for the 'shocking' elements of the blue door and the boy's blond hair that serve to contrast against the main character and her world.

◀ **Digital method** The page is coloured digitally, using a narrow palette. Digital colours are bright and excellent for reproduction.

Make sure that your roughs have brought you to the point where you are happy with the look of each page. Check the panels are in order, that each page is composed well and that your story flows well from panel to panel and from page to page. Is there still enough space for your dialogue, and are there areas of art that will be covered by balloons? Is your figurework believable, and, most of all, loose enough? At this stage one thing to keep in mind – and your drawing hand – is to try to keep some of the looseness of line work that was present in the early planning.

Technical proficiency isn't everything: readers will often respond better to an imperfect image that hums with energy than a pristine, highly accurate drawing that is rendered sterile by reworking. The most important part of pencilling is knowing when to put down pencil and eraser and declare a page finished. If in doubt, leave a page, go on to the next, and come back to it after a couple of days. You'll be able to spot any problems far more easily after getting some distance. When you are happy with your pencils, ink and colour them using your favoured methods.

Final piece ▲
Line work is finalized, inked and shaded, paying attention to line weight. The page is scanned and coloured on the computer, picking out a mood with the use of pale brown shades.

Tip: Before you declare a page finished, compare it with your original thumbnail. Hold your larger artwork at arm's length if need be. Has the energy and information contained in the thumbnail translated across? If not, is there anything you can do to fix it at the inking stage?

Whether you end up giving your pencils to another person to ink, as is the norm in larger 'creative teams' where time is of the essence, or you're going to do it yourself, get into the habit of marking the areas that will be completely filled with black with an 'X'. This saves you shading time at the pencilling stage and helps the inker, as most inks adhere better to the page when applied directly to bare paper.

Some artists who have become comfortable with tablet pens prefer to do their inking directly on to a computer, which, while fiddly, allows for much greater control over the line work and the ability to erase and redraw lines without having to use white-out or patch in new panels. However, inking via a software package such as Photoshop tends to produce rather stiff lines for artists beginning to explore the technique. If you want to give it a go, scan your pencils in at about 600 dpi for print resolution.

◀ Inks and colour
Inks tighten up the art for clearer reproduction, and add visual interest by differentiating foreground and background elements through different line widths. Colours influence mood, make changing time, scene and setting easier, and generate final artwork that is easier to read.

Roughs ▲
This page lays out all of the storytelling information and detail work in a clear, consistent manner. Balloon placements have been made, figures have been fully rendered, and the page is ready for inking. Your pencilwork may not be as tidy as this, but don't worry: that's what the inking stage is for!

Tip: Inks and colours should always be building on the clear storytelling you establish at the pencilling stage. It is possible to polish up your weaknesses, and it's equally true that bad inks and colours can ruin great pencils but clarity at the pencil stage pays dividends later.

Glossary

Archetypes Characters you would expect to find in a particular genre of story, without whom the story may be unable to progress. Archetypes include a young protagonist who is destined to become a hero, along with the old man who will become his mentor.

Background The items or characters in the rear of a panel or scene; the scenery created around characters.

Character A single active entity in your story. They can be human, alien, animal, monstrous or other: they count as long as they play a part whether large, small or cameo in a narrative.

Chibi Japanese word to describe characters that are shrunk into a small, cute, child-like form. This drawing style is sometimes called 'super-deformed'.

Comic A sequential narrative that uses a mixture of complimentary words and pictures to tell a story.

Cross-hatching A method of pen or pencil shading by which parallel lines are crossed over one another to form 'hatches'. The closer and more dense the lines, the darker the area.

Cyberpunk A genre that confronts the future potentials of technology and increasing prevalence of the internet in the modern world.

Dialogue The words spoken by characters during a story, shown on the page as the contents of 'speech balloons'.

Dip pen The most commonly used form of inking pen.

Focus This can be where the reader's eye is or should be directed in any particular panel or page, the most important element of a panel or page, or depth of field.

Font A lettering style used to write dialogue or sound effects.

Foreground Items or characters towards the front of a panel or scene.

Foreshortening The act of drawing items larger in a panel as they get closer to the 'camera' in order to exaggerate the perspective.

Focus lines Tightly spaced lines radiating out from the focal point of a panel to denote emotion, a shocking moment, or to highlight speed.

Graphic novel Either a book-length collection of existing, previously serialized material (*see* tankubon for the manga equivalent) or an entirely new, book-length sequential narrative.

Hero This can be a brave and noble man with great ability, or the main male character in a piece of fiction.

Heroine This can be a brave and noble woman with great ability or the main female character in a piece of fiction.

Highlight Bright areas of colour or grayscale applied on areas facing toward the main light source, in order to add depth to an image.

Hokusai A famous artist of ukiyo-e woodcuts, he was the first to use the term 'manga' in connection with illustrated scenes, in the title of one of his portfolios.

Indian ink The most commonly used form of ink: its consistency is perfect for use in dip pens and with brushes, and it is more resistant to light, heat and water than technical or writing pen inks when dry.

Inking The act of drawing over rough or finished pencils in black ink, tightening lines and adding shading, definition and texture in the process, to produce artwork that will scan, colour and reproduce more cleanly.

Jidaimono Japanese plays that feature historical plots and characters, often based around Samurai. The word is most often translated as 'period plays'.

Josei Manga created for late teenage and adult female audiences. They tend to be about the everyday experiences of women living in Japan.

Kodomo Manga aimed at younger children, often with an educational element, but always using attractive, cute characters, bright colours and uncomplicated dialogue.

Layout This can be the stage of page-creation when one sketches in the placement and size of the panels, and the major characters and features within them, or the placement of panels on the page.

Lettering The placement of dialogue and sound effects (SFX) on the page.

Line A mark long in proportion to its breadth, made with a pen, pencil or brush. 'Line art' is black ink lines on a white page.

Mahokka 'Magical girls': genre of shojo stories featuring girls with secret identities and special powers, who usually fight monsters and attend school at the same time.

Manga-ka The creator – or chief creator, in the case of a manga-ka who runs their own studio – of a manga.

Materials A catch-all term for anything used in the process of creating art.

Mecha Another term for the giant robots that populate many manga.

Meiji Era The 45-year rule of the Meiji Emperor, from 1868 to 1912, during which Japan began its modernization and ascended to the world stage, ending its isolationist policy.

Nib The tip of a pen, used to hold ink and transfer it to the page.

OEL (Original English Language) Manga produced by artists and writers in either the UK or US, following the stylistic conventions of Japanese manga in an entirely new, untranslated story.

Opaque Not transparent; a colour that obscures anything it is placed on top of.

Outline This can be the line surrounding a distinct shape or object, or the rough form of a story or plot.

Panel The basic building block of a manga page. Panels can be any size or shape, but each contain a single unit of action. The movement in a manga story happens in the 'gutters', or white areas in between each panel.

Pattern An image or series of colours that repeat or can be repeated.

Perspective The means by which 3D is simulated on the page, according to one or more vanishing points, to which all of the lines and objects in the panel or page diminish.

Protagonist The central character of a story and manga: they may not be a 'hero' in the traditional definition of the term, but the story is told from their viewpoint and readers follow their actions for the bulk of the narrative.

Quasi-historical A story set in a roughly historical period, i.e. Samurai-era Japan, without conforming to rigid historical events or personages.

Roughs A mocked-up or hastily sketched version of a page, in pencil.

Scene A unit of story, denoted by continuity of character or location.

Script The last result of the planning phase, when the contents of your panels are written as description and dialogue.

Seinen Manga aimed at older males, from late teens and up. Its themes may appear superficially similar to shonen, but it will include more explicit content.

Sentai Literally, a military unit, but in manga, it is often used to denote a squadron of characters who band together to pilot giant mecha.

SFX lettering Lettering designed to mimic a sound effect, in an onomatopaeic fashion. Any sound can receive SFX in this manner, from explosions and gunfire to blinking and breathing.

Shade This can be the mixture of a colour with black to reduce lightness, or synonym for 'colour'.

Shadow Darker areas of colour applied on areas facing away from the main light source, in order to add depth to an image.

Shojo Style of manga aimed at young and teen girls, with strong female protagonists. Can cover a multitude of genres, but romance and the emotional interior world are usually paramount.

Shonen Style of manga aimed at young and teen boys, with strong male protagonists and an emphasis on action and dominance of a particular field.

Shortlines A type of shading that uses very short, overlapping lines to suggest depth and shading.

Sketch A very rough drawing.

Soft shading A form of shading using multiple shades of the same colour, blended into one another. Unlike cel shading, soft shading uses multiple intermediate tones to create a more naturalistic effect.

Speech balloons (bubbles) Oval or elliptical white balloons that carry the dialogue of characters. A 'tail' points from the main balloon towards the relevant character's mouth.

Speedlines Tightly grouped lines radiating from or attached to a swiftly moving character in order to denote motion and relative speed. Focus lines can also be used to show a head-on character in motion.

Spokon A genre of manga in which the principal characters are athletes, and the majority of the stories revolve around a sport.

Steampunk A genre that takes the superficial trappings of cyberpunk and applies them to a quasi-19th century world, positing that computing and robotics were created in the age of steam and rivets, rather than the silicon age.

Stereotype A preconceived, oversimplified, demeaning and exaggerated assumption about a person or persons based on age, class, ethnicity, occupation, etc.

Stippling The use of tightly packed individual dots to create shading. The closer the dots are placed, the darker the shade.

Strip Any sequence of comic or manga images. In the West, it is most often used to refer to the four panel 'comic strips' found in newspapers, though the terms are largely interchangeable.

Super-deformed characters Characters exaggerated in their cuteness and diminutive stature, often lacking noses, fingers, and anything but the most rudimentary or comical details.

Tankubon The manga equivalent of graphic novels or trade paperbacks: book-length collections of manga stories previously serialized in a weekly or monthly manga magazine.

Technical pens These pens come in a wide variety of styles and nib thicknesses, and usually carry their own ink supply as cartridges.

Thumbnails Early draft layouts of pages, at diminutive sizes.

Tint This can be the mixture of a colour with white, to produce lightness, or synonym for 'colour'.

Tone A method of shading using pre-created patterns of moiré dots.

Tufts The bristled ends of paintbrushes, which come in a variety of styles, from pointed round to fan.

Viewpoint This can be the literal position from which a panel or page is drawn, the perspective through which a given story is filtered or told, or a philosophical, ideological or moral perspective.

Villain The central antagonist of a story, usually one who is dedicated to tearing down the life of the hero or heroine, or who is endangering the hero's family, city or world with their schemes.

Year 24 group A group of female manga-ka born in Showa 24, or 1949. They revolutionized the techniques and content of shojo manga, as well as marking the first time that shojo had been written and drawn, as well as read, by women.

Index